P9-CRQ-720

RICH MULLINS

His Life and Legacy

an Arrow Pointing
to Heaven

RICH MULLINS

His Life and Legacy

an Arrow Pointing to Heaven

James BRYAN Smith

BROADMAN
&HOLMAN
PUBLISHERS

Nashville, Tennessee

0-8054-2135-1

Published by Broadman & Holman Publishers, Nashville, Tennessee

Dewey Decimal Classification: 782
Subject Heading: BIOGRAPHY
Library of Congress Card Catalog Number: 00-037971

Published in association with the literary agency of
Alive Communications, Inc., 7680 Goddard Street, Suite 200,
Colorado Springs, CO 80920.

Library of Congress Cataloging-in-Publication Data
Smith, James Bryan.
    Rich Mullins : an arrow pointing to heaven / James Bryan Smith.
        p. cm.
    Includes bibliographical references.
    ISBN 0-8054-2135-1
    1. Mullins, Rich. 2. Contemporary Christian musicians—
United States—Biography. 3. Contemporary Christian music—
History and criticism. 4. Christian life. I. Title.
ML420.M7715 S65   2000
782.25—dc21
[B]

00-037971

2 3 4 5 04 03 02 01 00

To
John and Neva Mullins,
who gave faith hands
and feet and wings

c O N T e n t s

J esus of Nazareth ruined Rich Mullins's life.

And out of the ruins He recreated a ragamuffin of star-

tling originality; no human being who has crossed my

path even remotely resembles him.

Our first meeting took place in a ramshackle restaurant in Wichita, Kansas. We sat for three hours wolfing down drop-dead delicious profiteroles, chocolate pastries stuffed with vanilla ice cream. With a candor, humility, and raw honesty that reminded me of the tax collector in the temple, he laid out his life story with all the sin and failure that had scarred his soul, as well as the personal and professional successes that had established his reputation.

As he spoke I thought to myself, *This man knows the real Jesus. Only someone who has experienced the forgiveness and mercy of the redeeming Christ could dare to be so open about his brokenness.*

That "our God is an awesome God" is not something Rich read in a book or heard in a sermon. The God, bodied forth in Jesus, that he shares with us in his writings and his music is the God he encountered on the turf of his ragged journey.

Los Angeles poet Lynn Prescott caught his spirit when she wrote, "He was interested in gays and straights, whores and cowboys, alcoholics and people who were broken, broken, broken; he was interested in rainbow people and Franciscan vows; he had an appetite for sin but a voracious appetite for God. Action was his middle name. He had a short attention span and bored readily and quickly. In our day he would best be compared to a medieval troubadour/poet; he was largely a medievalist and not a renaissance man; he was a poet, pure and simple and as changing as the tides; he had many passions, and the ones he clung to most fiercely were his love for Native Americans, his love of Ireland and of children, his love of ragamuffins and of music; and lastly but not leastly, his passion that fired all other passions—his love for Jesus. Even dead and in his grave, Rich has helped me rediscover a lot of the pieces that I had lost; he helped me reclaim myself in a way that no human being has ever done."

Seven months before he died, I guided Rich on a three-day silent retreat at Chateau Vineyard, a resort sixty miles north of Atlanta. He was in a state of emotional turmoil because of unresolved issues with his family of origin, specifically his father. Like Henry Nouwen's dad, John Mullins loved his son but never told him so. He was truly proud of Rich's accomplishments, shared his deep affection for him with other members of the family but failed to communicate his feelings to the one person who longed for his love.

The two of us bonded here because my experience with my father matched his. When a father's love is withheld, a child will struggle with issues ranging from shyness and insecurity to a profound and crippling shame over his or her very existence. As Dennis Lynn notes, "As an adult, he or she may find it hard to accept compliments and attention and may even feel like hiding. Often such a person, no matter how conscientious and successful, will feel like a fraud and fear being found out. Or, on the other hand, a person whose (father) was not happy to discover him or her may compulsively seek compliments and attention throughout life without knowing why."

During the retreat I asked Rich to write a letter to his deceased father. The next day I asked him to write a letter from his father to him. Rich resided in the chalet next to mine. As he wrote I heard sobbing and wailing so loud that I started crying myself. All John Mullins's pent up affection exploded and came cascading into Rich's heart like a torrent of truth and love. Soon after, Rich came to my place and read the letter, tears streaming down his face.

Next I asked Rich to write a letter to Abba followed by a letter from Abba to him. I shall never forget our festive dinner on the last night of the retreat. His black eyes shining like onyx and his face creased in a radiant smile, he said simply, "Brennan, I'm free."

Much of his pain, as Jim Smith remarks, came from the fact that he saw too much and felt too much. His mother, Neva, said, "He could see the pain in another person even before they could see it themselves." Poets are a unique breed of human beings. They ricochet between agony and ecstasy because they take everything so personally. Where other people feel kicked by an unkind word, the poet feels disemboweled. The slightest provocation can induce a fit of weeping or a fit of ecstasy. Others cannot understand why he does what he does, and the poet is downright clueless himself. Rich Mullins often endured loneliness, as many people do, but he suffered in a way unknown to most of us. Such extraordinary sensitivity is a blessing and a heartache.

Rich taught me an invaluable lesson about the true meaning of repentance. One rainy day he got into a blistering argument with his road manager, Gay Quisenberry. Angry words were hurled back and forth, and Rich stormed out the door, uncontrite. Early the following morning, Gay was awakened from a sound sleep by the loud buzz of a motor outside her house. Groggily, she looked out the window and saw Rich mowing her lawn!

He never said he was sorry; he showed it. (It reminded me of a distraught woman who came to me for counseling. She had unfairly criticized her husband several times and feared it was becoming a pattern. Instead of telling her to recite the ancient prayer, "Lord Jesus Christ, Son of God, have mercy on me, a sinner," I asked her, "What is your husband's favorite dessert?" A bit disconcerted, she replied, "Carrot cake." I said, "Bake him two." Rich taught me to let the punishment fit the crime.

He walked the way of the ragamuffin. His vivid awareness of his own brokenness made it existentially impossible to sit in judgment on the sins of others. Rich disdained money and material things and secretly gave away most of what he earned. I carry this spirit with me to this day: one hidden act of kindness is worth more than all the burial mounds of rhetoric, all the mumbling and fumbling and tardiness of Christians so preoccupied with cultivating their prayer lives that they cannot hear the anguished cry of the child in the barrio.

Jim Smith has chosen wisely to eschew biography and hagiography in his presentation of Rich's life. He understands the difference between knowing *about* and really *knowing* Rich. Biography tells us a person's place of birth, family of origin, educational background, habits, physical appearance, and so forth—all those vital statistics so clinically cold that they tell us nothing of the man who lives and loves and walks with God. Hagiography or premature canonization would make Rich shudder.

Let me share a letter I received from someone in Canada:

Dear Brennan,

A year ago I wanted to die. I had accepted Jesus as my Savior when I was eight years old. And the years of living a loveless Christianity have taken their toll. A misfit, a failure and full of grief. I resented the day for arriving and cursed the length of the lonely night. I knew that God was punishing me for my lack of holiness and great works, and that he was ready to cast me into the Hell reserved for the ungodly.

It was God himself by divine appointment who put the music and video of Rich Mullins' "A Liturgy, a Legacy and a Ragamuffin Band" into my hands. That day, January 2, 1995, I met Jesus and my life changed 360 degrees. How does a heart change? How does something of no value become worth something? Even now in writing this letter, my eyes fill with tears.

But even more exciting is how his CD has changed other people's lives. It has been sent to Finland, England, Wales, Siberia, France and Ireland. The lady in Ireland was ready to end her life. She wrote me that she can't understand how God could work so powerfully through a man she's never met. She said that her days are getting brighter. My friend Paul came over from France. Clutching the CD in his hands and with tears running down his cheeks, he cried, "I have peace at last."

As his mentor and friend, I honor my brother as a creative artist and a gifted singer/songwriter, but I honor him even more for an identity that will endure long after all the applause has ceased and all the trophies have been laid down—Rich Mullins, a witness to Jesus Christ.

It is expected that the writer of the Foreword will offer a glowing recommendation for the book. Such is the custom. But in this case there is more. Truth be told, I have been stunned by the lyrical power of Rich's sung and written words and by Jim's lucid and inspiring commentary.

This book deserves to be read and reread. It is a treasure.

Brennan MANNING

New Orleans

a C K N o w l e d g m e n t s

A book like this comes about not by the work of one person but by the efforts of many. When a book contains biographical material, it involves even more people. I have many to thank for their contributions and help.

Acknowledgments

I want to begin by acknowledging my gratitude to the Mullins family: Neva Mullins, Debbie Garrett, Sharon Roberts, Lloyd Mullins, David Mullins, and Dick Lewis. I will be forever honored by your invitation for me to write this book. I pray that it lives up to your hopes.

Next, I want to thank my wonderful wife, Meghan, for her love and support and many sacrifices. Time spent on this book was time taken from her. Thank you, Meghan, for all you did to allow me the time to do this. And thank you for carefully reading the first drafts of each chapter and giving me good, honest feedback and great ideas. You are my joy and my inspiration. G. K. Chesterton said, "Angels can fly because they take themselves lightly." Thank you for being my angel.

I also want to thank my son, Jacob, who is now seven years old. I will always remember the day when you came up to my study after a long day of writing, and I asked you, "Jake, do you want to be a writer when you grow up?" You said, "No, Dad, you can't play with your kids very much when you write books. And besides, baseball players make more money." I know that I can never get back the time I could have had with you. Thanks for sharing your dad this past year and for making me laugh a lot.

In addition to the Mullins family, there were several key people who gave me a lot of material from which to glean. Kathy Sprinkle, Beth Lutz, Gary Rowe, and Sam Howard—all close friends of Rich's from his days in Zion and at Cincinnati Bible College—provided me a wealth of material. Maybe more important to me, along the way you gave me constant encouragement and inspiration. Thank you.

I also want to thank Sandy McMullen, who gave me hundreds of pages of original material from her own research into Rich's writings. Your work, Sandy, saved me at least a year in research. The book would not be what it is if not for you. Similarly, I want to thank Danl Blackwood, who connected me with Sandy and gave me the computer technology needed to access all of the material.

I would also like to thank Gay Quisenberry, Rich's longtime manager and friend, who gave a lot of her time to help me in the early stages, and Beaker, for giving me his own unique blessing as I began this project. Both of you were close to Rich, perhaps none closer, and I am grateful for your friendship.

I also want to acknowledge the way in which my colleagues and supervisors at Friends University helped to make this book possible. Sheryl Riney, Bob Dove, Leroy Brightup, and Biff Green helped me find a way to carve out the time to write this book. Your belief in the importance of this project gave me the inspiration I needed.

I want to thank Ronda Magness, who never stopped encouraging me and helped me, on her own time, to organize my schedule and set up interviews. It is a wonderful thing to have friends who believe in you more than you do.

I would also like to say thank you to two people who helped me in research: Jeremy Davis and Warren Farha, the owner of Eighth Day Books. Also, I want to thank Tim and Lori Gillach and Patrick Sehl Jr. for reading and giving feedback on some of the chapters and for providing strong encouragement along the way.

I want to give a special thanks to the Kid Brothers. Thanks to Mitch McVicker for driving to Wichita and spending two days with me. I know how much you have gone through and how much Rich meant to you. Your courage is an inspiration to me, but it is your tenderness that teaches me about God's love. Thanks to Michael Aukofer, for giving me one of the most touching interviews and for caring about Rich so deeply. Thanks to Eric Hauck for paying so much attention to Rich, soaking in his words, and meditating on them. I relied a great deal on your insights. Thank you, finally, to Matt Johnson, for spending so much time helping me understand. Your observant eyes helped me a great deal. Thank you all. Rich's investment in each of you is compounding daily.

I also want to thank Jim Dunning Jr. for his unfailing confidence in me and his wise counsel along the way. And I would like to thank Kathy Yanni, who caught a vision of what this book could be from the very start and helped to make sure we found the right publisher. Your heart is made of gold.

I want to thank the people at Broadman & Holman, who showed me from the first few minutes that you understood what this book ought to be and what it ought not to be. Thank you, Vicki Crumpton, for your editing skills and ability to see where I could not see.

I want to say a very special thank you to David Mullins. Your tender heart and strong faith were a great example to me. Thank you for reading each chapter and giving me good guidance. Your brother is no doubt very proud of you. Thank you for carrying on his work.

And thank you, Brennan Manning, for showing both Rich and me so much about God's love. You changed both of our lives. Thank you for writing the foreword to this book. I am deeply honored.

Finally, I want to thank those persons who took the time to let me interview them. The book would be severely diminished if not for their contributions. I list them in alphabetical order: Jimmie Abegg, Michael Aukofer, Tom Boothe, Gary Chapman, Ashley Cleveland, Billy Crockett, Roberta Croteau, Don Donahue, Jim Dunning Jr., Debbie Garrett, Amy Grant, Eric Hauck, Connie Hawk, Doris Howard, Sam Howard, Jennifer Jantz, Matt Johnson, Phil Keaggy, Wayne and Fran Kirkpatrick, Dick Lewis, Alyssa Loukota, Mark and Beth Lutz, Phil Madeira, Sherri McCready, Fr. Matt McGinnis, Mitch McVicker, Marita Meinerts, David Mullins, Lloyd Mullins, Neva Mullins, Ben Pearson, Gay Quisenberry, Sharon Roberts, Gary Rowe, Billy Sprague, and Kathy Sprinkle.

*"I don't know many
people who have died
and left so many people
saying, 'I need what
Rich Mullins's life brought
to the table, and
I don't know where else
to find it except in
looking at his life
and listening to what
he had to say.'"*

A m y   G r a n t

i N T R o d u c t i o n

Rich Mullins stood upon a hill among castle ruins in Ireland. His friend and photographer, Ben Pearson, was standing below. Ben called out, "Lift up your arms," and Rich raised his arms to shoulder level as if making a cross and said, "You mean, like Jesus?" Ben yelled up, "No, lower." Rich dropped his arms a little, and suddenly Ben saw something he did not expect. From a distance Rich looked like an arrow pointing toward the sky. Ben yelled, "You look like an arrow, man. An arrow pointing in the right direction." He snapped the picture. It would be the final picture of the last photo shoot for Rich and Ben.

It was more than a picture. It was the summation of a person's life, a symbol that said more about who he was than mere words can. Rich Mullins was a man who stood among the ruins—the ruins created by his own faults and failings, the ruins that result from the ravages of time. In the midst of the ruins he pointed to heaven, to the God who bundles our brokenness and heals our wounds. He felt the winds of heaven as he stood upon the stuff of earth and pointed, through his words and his music, to something larger than even our dreams. Rich Mullins was an arrow pointing to heaven.

Most people know him through his songs. He wrote and recorded dozens of hit songs in contemporary Christian music. If you meet someone who does not know Rich's name, simply mentioning the song "Awesome God" will usually result in a smile and a response such as, "Oh, I know that song. We sing it in our church." According to his peers in the Christian music industry—Amy Grant, Michael W. Smith, Gary Chapman, Phil Keaggy, and a host of others—Rich's songs are some of the most beautiful and inspiring ever written.

But what most people do not know is the person behind the lyrics and the music. I wish that Rich were here to tell you himself; I wish you had the chance to get to know him, to listen to what he had to say, and to see how he lived. Unfortunately, Rich died in a car accident on September 19, 1997. Unless you were able to spend time with him, to draw close enough to understand his thoughts and witness how he expressed them, see how he lived and listen to what he thought, his life is unknown to you. That is the reason for this book.

How This Book Came to Be

A year after Rich died, many people approached his family and said, "Someone ought to write a book about Rich." After a lot of discussion and debate as to whether or not it would be beneficial, the family agreed that his life merited being written about. In the fall of 1998, Rich's brother, David, asked if I would be interested in working on such a project. I was deeply honored. I was a close friend of Rich's during the final years of his life. We became friends in 1990, and he lived with my wife, Meghan, and me from 1992 to 1995. In 1995 Rich left to live and minister on a Navajo reservation in the Southwest, but in a sense, he never left our home. He returned every few months, leaving his scent of patchouli and a few of his belongings scattered throughout our house.

Rich lived with us during what I believe were some of the best times in his life. He had come to Wichita, Kansas, and was attending Friends University, a small, Christian, liberal arts college. Rich was finishing his degree in music education so he could teach music to children on a Native American reservation. He lived with his writing partner and close friend, David Strasser (better known as Beaker) in a small house in town. I began teaching at Friends the same year Rich enrolled. I can honestly say that having Rich Mullins in my religion classes was very intimidating. It was a little like having Einstein in your physics class. Most of the time I wanted to hand him the chalk and sit down and listen. Occasionally I did.

When Beaker got married, Rich needed a place to stay, and he asked if he could live in our attic apartment. We agreed, and soon he became a part of our family. During the two and a half years he was with us, Rich and I spent nearly every night (much to my wife's chagrin) sitting up and talking about God, life's meaning, the church, our favorite authors, and passages of the Bible we were laboring to understand. We would sometimes talk well into the night. I feel privileged to have been able to engage in these deep discussions.

What This Book Is Not, and What It Is

After visiting with Rich's family, I realized that any book written about Rich should not be a hagiography (an attempt to turn him into a saint) because Rich would be the first to say, "I am not perfect. Don't put me on a pedestal. I am just a ragamuffin. Look to God, not me." Nor should it be a biography (a chronological account of his life) because that, too, would focus more on Rich and less on what was important to him. And what was important to Rich—the most important thing in his life—was urging people to draw near to God.

When he gave people his autograph he always wrote, "Be God's." That was his signature statement. Many of us want to be "good," and Rich believed that being good was a noble pursuit. But the highest pursuit was not to be good, but to be God's. The best thing any of us can be is fully devoted to the God who loves us with a passionate, reckless, furious love. I began to see that the kind of book that would most honor Rich, and most help readers, would be the kind of book that pointed beyond the man himself.

This book attempts to look more at the wisdom than at the facts of a life. While it contains many stories about Rich's life, it contains more of Rich Mullins's own words, which are provocative and profound. What he had to say, combined with how he lived his life, is what is most challenging. My hope is that by letting his insights come forth, you will find yourself reflecting on your own life.

This book is best described as a devotional biography. It gives the reader an insight into Rich's life (the things he did, the places he went, the things he loved), but more importantly, it allows the reader a chance to learn what he thought. Also included are quotes from authors and saints who shaped Rich's life and faith along with insights and stories from interviews I conducted with his family and friends. Unless they are footnoted, all of the quotes came from those interviews.

In preparing to write this book, I was pleased to discover a wealth of Rich's words recorded in articles and interviews. After studying this material I began to notice ten themes that Rich spoke a great deal about: the importance of our families, the role of the church, the love of God, the person of Jesus, the beauty of creation, the struggle and pain we experience in life, the joy of living simply, the struggle with sin and temptation, the call to love one another, and the reality of death and bliss of eternal life. Each chapter centers on one of these themes.

No, It Is Changing Me

No one I have ever met has challenged me to "Be God's" like Rich Mullins. I will never lose pictures I have of him in my mind. I am a better person for having known him. After I began writing this book, I felt a sudden fear. I was afraid of only one thing—that I would be changed. My fear was well founded. I took a year out of my life to live, eat, breathe, and think about almost nothing but Rich Mullins, and in doing so I have been deeply moved.

I have been changed. I now look at my own family heritage with more awe and appreciation. My love for the church, even in its weaknesses, is deeper. I live more freely and joyfully in the "furious love of God," as Brennan Manning calls it. I cannot look at a tree or a star or a flower without praising God. I look at my own troubles, and the troubles of those around me, with a deeper appreciation because I know they are opportunities for growth. I have less interest in the things of this world. I am learning to look to Jesus and my friends for support when I feel the pull of sin. I view others with less judgment and more compassion. I am not as afraid of death, and I long for heaven more than I ever have. I would like to think that I am a little more of God's for having worked on this book.

Toward the end of his life Rich said, "I think we cry at funerals—even at funerals of people we don't like—because we realize what a miracle a life is. You realize, 'This will never happen again.' There will never be this exact combination of genes, there will never again be the things that have created this person to be what he is. God has spoken uniquely here, and it's gone. It's over. And I think there's some regret, because we all realize, boy, we didn't pay enough attention."[1]

This book is my attempt to help us pay attention to the uniqueness of Rich Mullins's life. God has spoken uniquely through his life and his words. Though Rich's life on earth has ended, his eternal life has just begun. As Dr. Steven Hooks said at Rich's memorial service, "There is a ragamuffin loose in heaven, and he is walking barefoot on the streets of gold." Until we reach the other side of the veil, we have his words and his music to help us on our own journey. It is my prayer that as you read this book you will come to know more about this man whose life, insights, and music were so powerful. But more than that, I hope you are somehow able to draw near to the God who made him who he was.

1

First Family

Understanding His Roots

Never picture perfect

Just a plain man and his wife

Who somehow knew

the value of hard work

good love and real life

Think, for a moment, about your lineage. Try to imagine your ancestors, at least two or three generations back. See if you can picture them. What did they look like, where did they live, and what did they do? Do you think it is possible that they ever dreamed of your existence one day in the future? What did they hope for, dream about? What hurt them? Did they ever fall in love, know heartache, savor joy?

Thinking about these questions forces us to realize that our ancestors were real people. A part of Rich's spiritual journey, and one that had a great effect on him, was the awareness of his own legacy. He was keenly interested in the coming to America of his great-great-grandparents, in his Irish/English/French heritage, and in his father's Appalachian upbringing.

In an interview Rich related:

A few generations back, there were twin brothers who were orphans in France. As young teenagers eager to find a better life, they stowed away on a ship bound for America. One of them was my great-great-grandfather. I remember the first time I flew into New York and saw the Statue of Liberty. I thought of those twins, my ancestors, both of them fifteen or sixteen years old, standing there on Ellis Island. They had come to begin a new life. They didn't even know the language. And I wondered what it felt like to them, years later, when they were eighty years old, with grandchildren, knowing that the dream of a better life had come true.

I remember, too, the first time I ever saw the Lincoln Memorial. I probably spent three or four hours sitting on the steps before I even went in to read the speeches. I'm not particularly patriotic, but that experience was just overwhelming. I don't know that the United States is "God's Country," but the church has been so strong here, and because of its influence, we hold life to be sacred and we believe that individuals have dignity. This is part of our legacy. I thought of this when I stood before the Lincoln Memorial, and when I saw the Statue of Liberty for the first time. Imagine the millions of people who have fled to America because of those very ideals. Somewhere back in my ancestry, from several different directions, people came to a country that was totally new. If any of them had not done that, I never would have happened. At least, I would not be who I have become.[1]

Pursuing Our Legacy

One of the first things we learn as children is our name. Our surname and our mother's maiden name become the dots through which we connect our past, as we discover the names and dates, births and deaths of those who went before us and somehow led to our being. But the people who form the branches of our family tree are more than names. Rich became interested in who they were, what they dreamed about, how they lived, and what they loved.

We carry in us the genes of a thousand men and women long gone. For many of us in America, those thousands of people came from other parts of the world. Even as a child Rich wanted to hear about these people. He said, "From when I was real little, I heard stories about people from Holland, people from Ireland, people from France, wherever our family came from."[2]

Some of us trace our roots hoping that one of our ancestors was a king or a queen or a famous hero. Much of the quest is fueled by pride, but for Rich the journey to find out where he came from actually had the opposite effect:

What I discovered is, heritage doesn't puff you up with pride. It really humbles you. If you look at the lives of the people you have come from you kind of go, "If they had married anyone else, if they had moved anywhere else, if their lives had been one iota different, I wouldn't be here." And so you have, not a big debt, not a crushing debt to pay, but you are part of an ongoing thing. You are not alone in the world. You are part of an ensemble.[3]

Rich discovered that his own life was the product of an amazing process of endless decisions made over countless centuries. If one of our ancestors had married a different person or died before giving birth to the next branch of the tree, we would not be here. This was a startling insight for Rich.

The Serendipity of Life

Rich grew up in a small town near Richmond, Indiana. Even the way his family ended up there was, for Rich, a serendipitous circumstance, an accident that would forever affect his life. He told the story this way:

My dad grew up back and forth between Kentucky and Virginia because his father was a coal miner. And when my dad was fourteen my grandpa came home and told my grandma to load up the truck 'cause they were gonna move. And when they took off they were going the wrong way—she just assumed they were going back to Virginia—and they were headed somewhere else. So my grandma said, "John, where in the world are we going?" And my grandpa said, "Well, Rose, we're going to Detroit." And she said, "Why in the world are we going to Detroit?" And he said, "Because I don't want my boys to grow up to be coal miners." And so they got as far as Indiana and ran out of gas—and that's how I got here.[4]

Not only are we dependent on whom our ancestors chose to marry; even the place we call home could depend on something as simple as how full a tank of gas was. The whole process was, for Rich, mystifying and humbling. Somehow, in the midst of the myriad decisions, God orchestrates our coming to be. Before the foundations of the earth were laid, the Scriptures tell us, God foreknew our existence, even through the happenstance of human choice (Eph. 1:4–5).

What is passed down to us determines much about our lives. Rich's maternal great-grandfather was a gifted man who was educated to be a doctor. But a series of events led him down a path into alcoholism. Unable to function as a doctor, he worked at different jobs but sometimes disappeared for weeks at a time, leaving his oldest son (Rich's grandfather) to take care of his family.

Commenting on this, Rich said in an interview, "A legacy is something that is passed on to you that you have no control over. I had no say in that my great-grandpa was an alcoholic. I had no say in the fact that my grandpa and grandma moved from Kentucky to Indiana. . . . There are all kinds of things that are pushed on us and we have no say over, and they shape the way we see everything."[5]

Despite our insistence that we are self-made men and women, we are dependent creatures. We like to think that we determine our destiny, but in reality we have very little to do with it. The people who raise us, our parents and our older siblings and our extended family, have tremendous influence on who we become.

The Bible is full of genealogies. Though we may find them dull, dry reading, they are there for a reason. The writers knew something we easily forget: that we are a part of an ongoing process, that we are dependent on others for our existence, and that our identity is related to genealogy. The blood of our great-great-grandparents flows through our veins, and a part of them continues on in us.

> *The family was ordained of God, that children might be trained up for himself. The family was before the Church, or rather, the first form of the Church.*
>
> — P o p e   L e o   X I I I

Mom and Dad

No one influences our lives as much as our parents. Rich was born Richard Wayne Mullins on October 21, 1955, to John and Neva Mullins in a small town in Indiana, near Richmond. His family called him Wayne. Though his first name was Richard, he went by the name Wayne until he went to college. Friends there called him Richard. When he began his music career, he became simply Rich. He insisted, though, throughout his life, that his family still call him Wayne. On one visit home a niece greeted him by saying, "Hi, Uncle Rich," and he gently reprimanded her, saying, "When I am with you, my name is Wayne." It was his way of guarding his family identity and staying connected to his roots.

Neva Mullins is a quiet woman with a reputation for godliness. She comes from a long line of Quakers, a denomination that focuses on silence, simplicity, and nonviolence. Rich's father, John Mullins, who died in the spring of 1991, was well-known for his hard work and honesty. Having grown up the son of an Appalachian coal miner, he learned quickly that life is difficult and not kind to the fainthearted. He was raised in the Christian church, a movement that emphasizes the authority of the Bible, hymn singing, and weekly Communion.

Rich had a very close relationship with his mother. In her he saw many of the ideals he longed for. She was kind and nurturing, and though very intelligent, she was not outspoken and rarely raised her voice or spoke an unkind word. Rich recalled how his mother was friendly toward an eccentric woman.

"You know, I have a great mom. It is just wild that this woman and my mom are friends. I asked, 'Do you ever feel weird around her?' and my mom said, 'Yeah, sure I do!' But here's the deal: No one was ever won into the kingdom of God through snobbery. We come to know Christ through love. I really believe that."[6]

His mother's love won Rich into the kingdom as well. In fact, all of the Mullins siblings attest to the power of Neva's faith and commitment in their lives. Rich's sister, Debbie Garrett, says, "She gave me birth, but she also gave me Life, life with God." Neva's gentleness and desire to be holy were two qualities that dramatically influenced Rich.

John Mullins worked with his hands, first as a tool and dye maker, then spending the latter part of his career running a nursery. Rich admired his father, who grew up in difficult circumstances, and was curious about his dad's Appalachian upbringing. He labored to understand this man who was, on the surface, very different from him. Rich said:

> My dad was an Appalachian, which is a very polite way to say that he was a hillbilly, and in junior high I was always embarrassed about my dad. He never dressed right, he never had a suit that fit him, and always had dirt or grease under his fingernails. In my junior year of high school we went to a funeral in Kentucky where my dad had grown up. My dad, who wasn't a sentimental, gushy kind of guy, pulled off the road. We walked around for a bit, and my dad said, "This is all changed. Somewhere out here there was a swimming hole and a vine we used to swing out over the water on." And I suddenly realized that my dad had been a kid once. At the time the most convicting verse in the Bible was "Honor your father and mother." And I realize now that that verse means that if you cannot honor your father and mother then you can't honor anybody. Until you come to terms with your heritage you'll never be at peace with yourself. That was a real breakthrough moment for me. So, what I needed to do was come to understand the Appalachian life, so that I could know more about my father, who had been a stranger to me all my life.[7]

As a way to gain understanding of his father's Appalachian heritage, Rich purchased a hammered dulcimer and quickly learned how to play it. In the years to come, that instrument became a key part of much of his music.

It is a strange awakening to discover that our parents were once children, that they were lonely and afraid and unsure of themselves. It helped Rich to realize that much of what he could not understand about his father could be explained by looking at where he came from. It is a healthy moment in our lives when we realize that our parents are human beings.

Rich appreciated his father's work ethic and especially his unpretentiousness: "My dad was very honest about who he was [and] . . . his weaknesses and strengths. He never pretended to be something he wasn't."[8] Most who knew Rich agree that if he had one outstanding quality, it was honesty. Sometimes Rich was painfully blunt. He had a kind of courage that allowed him to be vulnerable. This quality that he saw in his father, perhaps more than any other, became a very real part of Rich.

After they discovered Rich's love for music and obvious gifts, his father was the first to insist that he receive music lessons, and he worked hard to pay for them. His mother also did whatever she could to make sure Rich got the necessary training. She went without a coat one winter in order to pay for his piano lessons. When asked about this story, she replied, "Well, I probably didn't need a coat that much."

Rich said of his mom and dad:

I think my parents were really smart parents. I think they were, actually, pretty progressive for the time. The one thing that they really wanted me to know is what makes me tick, what I am about, how I approach life. And I think what my parents really wanted for me was for me to be who I am. I think a lot of parents hand people over a blueprint and say, "This is how you're supposed to do it." And my parents, I think, kind of drew a picture and said, "Here's the good stuff in life. How do you get there?"[9]

For his parents' fortieth wedding anniversary, Rich wrote a song. In it one can sense his appreciation for them and for the impact his early home life had on him.

First Family

My folks they were always the first family to arrive
With seven people jammed into a car that seated five
There was one bathroom to bathe and shave in

Six of us stood in line
And hot water for only three
But we all did just fine

Talk about your miracles
Talk about your faith
My dad he could make things grow
Out of Indiana clay
Mom could make a gourmet meal
Out of just cornbread and beans
And they worked to give faith hands and feet
And somehow gave it wings

I can still hear my dad cussin'
He's working late out in the barn
The spring planting is coming
And the tractors just won't run
Mom she's done the laundry
I can see it waving on the line
Now they've stayed together
Through the pain and the strain of those times

And now they've raised five children
One winter they lost a son
But the pain didn't leave them crippled
And the scars have made them strong
Never picture perfect
Just a plain man and his wife
Who somehow knew the value
Of hard work good love and real life

Talk about your miracles
Talk about your faith
My dad he could make things grow
Out of Indiana clay
Mom could make a gourmet meal
Out of just cornbread and beans
And they worked to give faith hands and feet
And somehow gave it wings

John apparently liked the song very much, but one day he turned to Neva and said, "How come you get to be described as the one making gourmet meals, and I am the one out cussing in the barn?"

Neva replied, "The truth hurts, doesn't it, honey?"

As related in the song, John and Neva Mullins raised five children and lost one, Brian, to spinal meningitis when he was only a few months old. Rich was only two at the time of Brian's death, but as he grew he admired how "the pain didn't leave them crippled," and in fact, the scars "made them strong." John and Neva, "just a plain man and his wife," gave Rich faith and a steady example of strength and godliness put to work.

The Bible gives us a commandment and a promise concerning our parents: "Honor your father and your mother, so that your days may be long in the land that the LORD your God is giving you" (Exod. 20:12). Rich found it easy to honor his mother because he had a deep respect for her and he constantly felt her love. But he found it difficult to honor his father during his teenage years even though he admired him, primarily because his father had difficulty communicating his love for him. Neva explains, "John's generation of men did not express their feelings to their children. As long as they didn't say anything to you, you were OK. It was the mothers who expressed love for their children . . . not the men in those days. I think it is a great thing that this has changed."

Very few people have "perfect parents." They are human beings, which is a way of saying that they, too, can be shortsighted and petty, that they are not all-knowing and all-seeing, that they can be as selfish and sinful as the next person. Why would God command us to honor them? The command to honor them has to do with the fact that, like it or not, they are the parents God gave us, and to honor them is, in a sense, to honor God. It is to live in the awareness of our dependence, which is the death of pride. In short, it is coming into the right order of life.

God created the system we call the family. It is his design, and in order for it to work properly, parents are to train and care for their children; children, in turn, are called to honor and obey their parents. When these two things are happening, there is harmony. When either or both of these are missing, there is chaos. Always. The command to honor our parents is not a painful burden but a prescription for happiness. That is why the commandment carries with it a promise: "Honor your father and your mother, so that your days may be long in the land that the LORD your God is giving you."

Rich's father could never tell him that he loved him, and this made Rich feel angry and distant. But the trip they took to Kentucky helped Rich to see his father as a human being, as one who was once a kid, as one who was the product of his environment. Rich realized that even though he didn't verbalize it, perhaps his dad really did love him. It was just not something he was trained to do.

Though the two had a difficult relationship, later in his life Rich made peace with his father. Rich went on a private retreat with Brennan Manning during the last year of Rich's life. Brennan gave him several exercises to do, including writing a letter to his father and writing a letter as if his father were writing it to him. This was the most healing event of Rich's life, he told me later. When he wrote two words—coming from his father—"Dear Wayne," he began sobbing uncontrollably. On the following pages is the letter he wrote as if from his father.

> *What is a home?*
> *It is the laughter of a*
> *child, the song of a*
> *mother, the strength of a*
> *father. Home is the first*
> *school, and the first*
> *church, where they learn*
> *about a loving God.*
>
> — E r n e s t i n e
> S c h u m a n n - H e i n k

Neva recalls, "When Wayne left home, he grew his hair out and often had a ponytail. His dad did not like it at all, and sometimes they fought about it. Eventually they just stopped talking about it.

"Several years later John and I went to a concert, and Wayne didn't know we were there. John came up from behind him and gently tugged on his ponytail. Wayne turned around and saw his dad smiling at him. Wayne told me that it was at that moment that he knew his dad loved and accepted him. That was a real turning point for the both of them."

It is a glorious thing to think about Rich and his father in heaven. I am certain that John was the first to meet Rich when he entered the gates, and I imagine that his father hugged him long and hard. Maybe he even came up from behind and tugged on his ponytail.

Dear Wayne

It's a lot like I told you "being poor aint shameful—just inconvenient." That's true with money and with knowledge and courage and everything else too. Where I was poorest was where it was most inconvenient for you. I could not imagine that people were as different as I no longer have to imagine. And because I couldn't imagine that sounds and rhythms and feelings and thoughts could be to you what machinery and calves and corn was to me—because I had no time to feel things and a quicker head than heart I never guessed that those things were valuable. But I valued you—it's just that I didn't know you. I tried to fit you in my armour and you had to face Goliath with a sling. Then I was embarrassed because of my blunder. I didn't know I was supposed to be affectionate—I thought that was soft. I thought a man had to be hard. I could see the strength of steel but I couldn't see the power of tenderness, or the courage it takes to hold tenderness up to a fire. When I compared you with others I didn't know the devil had his finger on the scale, or that he used my unimaginativeness to put it there. That may not even be a word but then you're the writer—I'm not and couldn't never be. Anyway—I can't even remember that you walked funny and had scrawny shoulders—did you? Who the hell cares.

There's that one movie you liked—I never liked movies all that much but I do more now. And in that movie some psychologist (something else I couldn't hardly stomach that I've gotten over—you won't believe what all you get over when you die) talked about how passion come out of a greek word that meant "pain." And he said he didn't want to kill that boys "passion"—to remove his "pain" because it was his passion. Well, I'm sorry for being the occasion for your pain, but it is yours now and there's a lot of it that got around. I am here in the company of several fathers who occasioned pain in their sons — Abraham did it to Isaac, Isaac did it to 10 of his sons, Noah did it to Ham, David did it to Absolom, God Almighty even did it to His boy Jesus. If you love someone you'll surely hurt them — that's a fact of life.

Be brave in your pain. I don't say that because you're not. I am proud that you didn't run off from it. But, keep brave — not like old Saul up here (who, by the way really wrecked Jonathon) — not by putting on the tough skin, the heavy armour — brave it out with the lightness of a sling whirled round — moving, vulnerable as all hell, graceful as the sun in skates. I was strong enough to stand — you be strong enough to fly. Passion — pain — don't have to wreck your life unless you make it. Then that's your choice

I once wrote you "October 21ᵗ, 1955 Richard made me a very proud man. And many times since that too." It was not enough but it was sincere. I'm up here in this cloud of witnesses and you can ask any of them, I brag about you all the time till they're about to kick me out. You are my passion — no less than my other kids — I thought I could love without being hurt, but love has broke me to pieces and every piece of me — every muscle — sings out "halelujah." Love is light and alive and don't come without pain. But the pain of love — that passion — it's the pain of longing, the hunger and thirst for righteousness. You should see how good righteousness looks on me. Your mother will faint. Now I look at it on you and weep for joy — I burst with it. Know that, and that

I love you,   your Dad

Discovering His Loves: *Music and the Church*

One of the ways we learn to survive in the world is to discover our unique-ness, our talents, and our gifts. For Rich, music would become a passion. He would work out his pain, as well as his highest aspirations, through music. He showed unusual musical abilities from an early age.

Rich's sister, Debbie, describes the first time they realized he had musi-cal gifts: "When I was about ten years old and Wayne was four or five, I was taking piano lessons. My teacher told me to practice the hymn, 'Abide with Me,' and I played it over and over but kept messing up on the same part. I got up to go into another room. Mom had been listening all the while as she was working in the kitchen. The next thing she heard was the hymn being played without a mistake, and she said, 'Oh, Debbie, you're really getting it.' She walked into the room, and there was little Wayne playing the song. He had been sitting there listening to me practice it for so long that he knew how it was supposed to be played."

From when I was real little, I always liked music. My great-grandpar-ents lived right next door to us and they had a piano, and I would go over all the time and play. And—I think my dad didn't want me to get in-volved in it totally because he wanted me to be a jock. And, like, there was just no way that was gonna happen. So I think he finally just gave up. Then, in elementary school he let me take piano lessons as a conso-lation prize. And actually the consolation prize turned out better than the grand prize.[10]

Sometimes our parents have an agenda for us that does not fit who we are. Rich's father was a farmer and an athlete, so it made sense that he would ex-pect his son to be the same. It was probably difficult for John to have a son who had a passion for something that was foreign to him.

Rich was not particularly good at farm work. Every member of the family has a story to tell about his ineptness. Once when he was riding the tractor, the wheel inexplicably fell off. Another time, his father had dug several holes in which to plant trees. While driving through that part of the field, Rich managed to get not one but all four wheels stuck in holes. His dad had to tow him out. Rich simply had no real mechanical skills. He wanted to be a good farmer and athlete; it simply wasn't in him.

As his mother puts it, "He just had music in him. He had to play." They eventually arranged for him to take piano lessons from a woman who would have a great impact on him. She helped Rich develop an overall understanding of music, why it is important to God and how it ought to be played. He described that relationship:

I had a very good music teacher, Mary Kellner, who not only introduced me to some of the great composers, but she was able to capture my imagination and make me excited about what I was supposed to be learning. When I was in fourth grade, I got asked to play the communion meditation at church. I practiced and she worked with me, which was cool because she was Quaker, and they don't even have communion. Anyway, I went back Tuesday to my lesson after I had played Sunday, and she said, "How did you do?" and I told her, "Everybody said they loved it, everyone said I did great." And she said, "Well, then you failed." I was crushed, but she put her hand on my shoulder and said, "Richard, when you play in church, you are to direct people's attention to God, not to your playing."[11]

That experience shaped the way Rich looked at music, especially in church. For the rest of his life, if asked to play in church, Rich would lead worship but never perform for fear of drawing attention to himself.

Rich's family discovered that he had another unique love: the church. Neva says, "There were two things I never had to tell Wayne to do: practice the piano and go to church." Even as a little boy, Rich came home and retold all of the stories he had learned. His sisters marveled at his ability to understand the preacher's sermons. He could recite parts of each sermon in detail.

While most children want to grow up and do something exciting or heroic, Rich wanted to follow God. His sister, Debbie, said, "Wayne was a funny kind of kid. . . . When you asked him what he wanted to be when he grew up, he said he wanted to be a missionary. . . . No policeman, no fireman, he wanted to be a missionary."[12]

Rich learned a lot about the Christian faith from his extended family, particularly his great-grandmother, whom he described as "a wonderful woman [who] had a very down-to-earth approach to religion. She said bad words sometimes, and I loved that. That's why I always liked Christmas—because it was the only time you could say 'ass' in church. I used to sing that line out of that carol over and over again."[13]

Rich often described his family tree as being filled with "a bunch of heavenly saints and a few notorious sinners." He believed that our families teach us about life by their example. If their lives are exemplary, we see in them certain virtues that we would like to cultivate. If their lives go badly, it may be that we try to shun the vices that spelled their demise. Either way, they—both the saints and the sinners—represent all of humanity and are in a sense a microcosm of the world.

The early years of Rich's life were shaped by great-grandmothers, uncles, cousins, and all kinds of people who in their own way communicated the faith. But he would learn that his faith would not make life easy.

Adolescence: *The Outsider*

During his teenage years, Rich struggled to fit in. He was raised in Indiana, a state known for basketball and farming, and Rich was not good at either. Musical proficiency and spiritual understanding were not high on the popularity list. Consequently Rich was shy. As he noted in later years, "I have no physical genius about me. I can't dribble a ball and run at the same time, I can't do lay-ups—I'm not an athlete. But my experience as a kid was, I was made fun of so much that what I did then, is, I wouldn't participate. And I think I cheated myself out of a lot of fun."[14]

Rich further reflected in a radio interview:

When I was young, I was angry and I was kind of going, "God, why am I such a freak? Why couldn't I have been a good basketball player? I wanted to be a jock or something. Instead I'm a musician. I feel like such a sissy all the time. Why couldn't I be just like a regular guy?" The more I thought about it, the more I realized that, you know, sometimes God has things in mind for us that we can't even imagine. And I think that maybe it was good for me to grow up being picked on a little bit, because then I realized what it meant to be kinda the underdog. And then to have someone who is not an underdog, someone like God, say, "Hey, I want you to be with Me," then you kinda go, "Wow!" And so maybe for that reason, grace is more important to me than people who have been able to be more self-sufficient.[15]

Not fitting in forced Rich to shy away from a lot of typical activities growing up. Our peers can be ruthless with their teasing, and the common result is that we stop trying to fit in altogether and carve out a niche that suits our talents, but we miss out on a lot.

Yet Rich had trouble fitting in with religious types too. He was too saintly for the sinners and too sinful for the saints. He was always active in the

> *The family is a good institution because it is uncongenial. It is wholesome precisely because it contains so many divergences and varieties. It is like a little kingdom, and, like most other little kingdoms, is generally in a state of something resembling anarchy. Aunt So and So is unreasonable, like mankind. Papa is excitable, like mankind. Our youngest brother is mischievous, like mankind. Grandpa is stupid, like the world; he is old, like the world.*
>
> — G. K. Chesterton

church, which made it difficult to fit in with the non-Christian crowd. But Rich was always searching and questioning, and he liked to bash people's sacred cows, which made it difficult to fit in with the Christians. In later years he reflected: "It seems that I always am and always have been an outsider. I've never really fit in. I was always too religious for my rowdy friends—they thought I was unbelievably hung up—and too rowdy for my religious friends—they were always praying for me."[16]

Finding His Place

Though Rich had trouble fitting in on the farm or the basketball court, he was always comfortable behind a piano. His sister, Sharon, sang in an all-county choir that had lost its accompanist. She told the director that she had a brother who could play for them, and the director agreed to let him try out. When Rich showed up for the audition, the director gasped. Rich was only thirteen years old, but he proceeded to astonish the director and the whole choir with his skills. He could play anything and play it well. The only criticism he received was that he improvised too much.

Rich went on to create and lead a touring ensemble he formed from within that group called Children of the Light, though he was only sixteen at the time. Rich wrote many of the songs himself, and the six-member group played in churches throughout the region. During this period he began to write songs with real seriousness, and his passion for music seemed to increase each day.

When Rich was a senior in high school, he spent his free time practicing piano in the sanctuary of his church. Just before graduation, he cut his afternoon classes to practice. A teacher saw him and informed the principal, who in turn called his mother. They threatened not to let him participate in his commencement ceremony but later relented.

> *When I was a boy of fourteen, my father was so ignorant I could hardly stand to have the old man around. But when I got to be twenty-one, I was astonished at how much he had learned in seven years.*
>
> — Mark Twain

After graduation Rich attended Cincinnati Bible College. There he formed a small Christian band called Zion. The group played at colleges and led retreats in Indiana, Kentucky, and Ohio. Rich recorded his first album with Zion. His next home would be Nashville and later Wichita. His final earthly home was on a reservation in New Mexico. Rich never put down many roots. He sometimes referred to himself as a "homeless man" in the same sense that Jesus, too, was a man "who did not have a home."

Home

Rich's musical gifts took him all over the world, but he often stopped in Richmond to see his family. During one of his last visits with his mother, in the summer of 1997, he said as he was about to leave, "Well, I gotta go home." She asked him where "home" was, and Rich told her he really couldn't answer that. In his earthly life, even with all of the accolades and attention he received, he was never quite at home. His sister, Debbie, says, "The audiences applauded for Rich, but what he wanted was to be loved as Wayne."

Our parents create an environment in which we can grow. We call it the home. The home is the most powerful place on earth. It is the cradle of the soul. Our minds and personalities, our loves and our hates, our fears and our dreams are all molded in the home. The home is the workshop of God, where the process of character-making is silently, lovingly, imperceptibly carried on. We search throughout our lives for love and identity, and if we are fortunate, we may find it.

The quest for our identity will always lead us back to our families. They are the ones with whom we discover our potential, as well as our limitations. They are the ones through whom and with whom we learn how to live. It is sheer hubris to think that we are "self-made" women and men. We learn how to live from other people. We did not develop in a vacuum, we were taught how to function from other people and by no one more so than our parents and our siblings. Rich's family shaped him, and he in turn shaped them.

We have families because we are weak creatures, and God knows that we need them. Throughout our lives, those people who knew us first are a part of our makeup even if they are difficult to live with. Old men and women can see their parents in their minds as if it were yesterday. Even in his last years, Rich could still picture his dad cussing in the barn and managing to grow plants out of the tough Indiana clay. He could see his mom hanging laundry and taste her cornbread and beans. Jamming seven people into a car that seats five may not be comfortable, but it is family. In terms of soul-shaping, it is the most powerful place in the world.

2

Creed

Being Made in the Church

And I believe that
what I believe
Is what makes me what I am
I did not make it,
no it is making me
It is the very truth of God
and not the invention of any man

R ich Mullins loved the church. He was nurtured in it, learning there the truths of his faith that would shape him. He did not believe that we go to church because we are perfect; he believed that we go to church because we need it. He looked at the Christian life as a process, an ongoing struggle to be faithful to what we know is true. And he understood that we are prone to failure and therefore in need of the support, direction, and accountability found only in the church.

I hear people say, "Why do you want to go to church? They are all just hypocrites." I never understood why going to church made you a hypocrite because nobody goes to church because they're perfect. If you've got it all together, you don't need to go. You can go jogging with all the other perfect people on Sunday morning. Every time you go to church, you're confessing again to yourself, to your family, to the people you pass on the way there, to the people who will greet you there, that you don't have it all together, and that you need their support. You need their direction. You need some accountability, you need some help.[1]

Rich believed that the Christian life is not a one-time faith commitment and then merely a long wait until we die. We need constant sustenance; we cannot live off of the momentum of our past. He and Beaker wrote a song that expressed that never-ending need:

Step by Step

Oh God You are my God
and I will ever praise You

Oh God You are my God and I will ever praise You
I will seek You in the morning
And I will learn to walk in Your ways
And step by step You'll lead me
And I will follow You all of my days

Rich later commented on the song:

With "Step by Step," if I had to make an overall statement, it's that faith is walking with God. The biggest problem with life is that it's just daily. You can never get so healthy that you don't have to continue to eat right. Because every day I have to make the right choices about what I eat and how much exercise I need. Spiritually we're in much the same place. I go on these binges where it's like "I'm going to memorize the five books of Moses." I expect to be able to live off the momentum. The only thing that praying today is good for is today. So, with "Step by Step" . . . it's not what you did, and not what you say you're going to do, it's what you do today.[2]

Rich was very aware of the constant need for spiritual nourishment, which is why he sought the support of Christian friends throughout his life and believed in the need for the church.

From the beginning of his life, Rich was connected to the church. His mother took him and his two sisters to Quaker meetings every week until he was six years old. Though Rich attended Whitewater Christian Church through all his later growing-up years, he never forgot the formative experience of Quaker worship and its unique dimensions (the immediacy of God's presence, silence, and simplicity in lifestyle). This was a very formative experience for Rich. He spent time in the presence of devout men and women who gathered together to be in silence, to hear the Word, and to be open to the Spirit, who is alive and present. Rich came to believe that being in the company of the committed is one of the most transforming agents God has given us.

At church Rich was exposed to the Bible, and he loved Bible stories. He memorized the stories he heard in Sunday school. The church is also where he learned how to pray. When asked in an online interview, "How do you keep your faith in the Lord so strong?" he answered with a children's verse he had been taught in Sunday school: "Read your Bible, pray everyday and you'll grow, grow, grow."[3]

Marita Meinerts worked for a time as one of Rich's tour managers and became a good friend. She said, "He talked about church, his roots, and his upbringing, but he realized that his foundation of what he thought about God started early on. He said in some of his concerts that he wondered as a kid why we couldn't get more wine and bread because he was hungry. And he used that memory to talk about how we hunger for communion in a spiritual way."

Rich hungered for God and he found what he needed in the church. He was aware that many people try to find other ways to satisfy that hunger, none of which, he believed, can replace what the church has to offer. One common substitute he saw often was trying to live off of emotional experiences, like listening to Christian music. He said pointedly, "People . . . take it so seriously. I'm in contemporary Christian music, and I don't know nothing. If you want spiritual nourishment, go to church."[4]

He was afraid that many people listened to his music as a means of spiritual growth, when in fact he believed his music to be simply entertainment. He would become very discouraged that people knew more lines from his songs than they did from the Scriptures.

Sometimes it concerns me, the number of people who can quote my songs, or they can quote the songs of several different people, but they can't quote the Scriptures—as if anything a musician might have to say would be worth listening to. Really, I mean, what musicians do is they put together chords, and rhythms, and melodies. So if you want entertainment, I suggest Christian entertainment, because I think it's good. But if you want spiritual nourishment, I suggest you go to church or read your Bible. . . . The Christian music industry is a capitalistic endeavor, period. And if anyone is interested in spiritual vitality they need to invest themselves in a church, not in an industry.[5]

Though he recognized the limitations of the Christian music industry, Rich was careful not to be too critical of it; it was his vocation and a calling he embraced. He did not, however, want people to make the mistake of thinking that being entertained by music could replace being transformed by being part of a local church.

The Eternal Truths

Rich knew that his music came from his own ideas, and however inspired, they were still transient and feeble compared to the teaching of the church. The church contained something "more eternal." Rich said, "Our faith becomes real when we focus on what never changes instead of our ever-changing opinions."[6] There is something, he said, that is "higher than the songs that I can sing."

> *He cannot have God for his Father who refuses to have the Church for his Mother.*
>
> — Saint Augustine

There is a wonderful word to describe the classic doctrines of the church: *orthodox*. The roots *ortho*, meaning right or correct, and *dox*, meaning glory or worship combine to mean "the right glory" or "the correct way to worship." Orthodoxy was an important idea for Rich. He believed that the world around us is trying to fill us with its own version of the truth, but the church alone stands against the culture because it contains the Truth, the only truth about God, about Jesus, about the Spirit, and about human beings and their destiny.

As a member of the body of Christ, Rich felt bombarded by the lies of the world ("man is just an evolved animal" or "happiness is found in wealth") and longed to anchor his life in unchanging truths. He sought this in the church.

When I go to church, . . . I involve myself in something that identifies me with Augustine, that identifies me with Christ, that identifies me with nearly 2000 years of people who have come together once a week and said, "Let's go to the Lord's table and enjoy the feast that He has prepared for us." In that week I may have been subjected to a million billboards that try to make me identify with the thinking of contemporary society. But once a week I go back to church, and acknowledge that though the shape of the world is really different now than it used to be, this remains the same: I still come to the Lord's table and say, "Oh God, if it weren't for your grace, if it weren't for the sacrifice of Christ, my life would have no meaning, no life would have real substance." And I do that voluntarily.[7]

The unchanging truths are the possession of the church. God has made the church the steward of orthodoxy, and she has fought for centuries to bring those truths to us. We are indebted to the women and men who labored to make sure the message that was given to the apostles made its way to you and me.

That is why one of Rich's most powerful songs, and one he enjoyed singing in concert more than any other, is "Creed." As his friend and fellow musician, Phil Madeira, said, "I think everything that was important to Rich was wrapped up in . . . 'Creed.'"

Creed

I believe in God the Father
Almighty Maker of Heaven and Maker of Earth
And in Jesus Christ His only begotten Son, our Lord
He was conceived by the Holy Spirit,
Born of the virgin Mary,
Suffered under Pontius Pilate,
He was crucified and dead and buried

And I believe that what I believe is what makes me what I am
I did not make it, no it is making me
It is the very truth of God and not the invention of any man

I believe that He who suffered was crucified, buried and dead
He descended into hell and on the third day, He rose again
He ascended into Heaven where He sits at God's mighty right hand
I believe that He's returning
To judge the quick and the dead of the sons of men

I believe in God the Father
Almighty Maker of Heaven and Maker of Earth
And in Jesus Christ His only begotten Son, our Lord
I believe in the Holy Spirit
One Holy Church
The communion of Saints
The forgiveness of sins

I believe in the resurrection,
I believe in a life that never ends

And I believe that what I believe is what makes me what I am
I did not make it, no it is making me
It is the very truth of God and not the invention of any man

Rich and Beaker wrote the song on an airplane during the time Rich was recording the album *A Liturgy, A Legacy and a Ragamuffin Band*. Rich needed one more song for the album, and he had been influenced by a line from G. K. Chesterton's book, *Orthodoxy*. Chesterton stated in the beginning of the book that the orthodoxy he hoped to convey was not his invention, but rather that "God and humanity made it; and it made me."[8] Orthodoxy, wrote Chesterton, is to be found in the Apostle's Creed, and the entire book was his attempt to bring those truths to the modern reader once again.

Rich attempted the same with "Creed." He took the words of the Apostle's Creed, spoken in many churches across the country—Protestant and Catholic—each week, and put them to music. The refrain contains his own version of the line by Chesterton: "And I believe what I believe is what makes me what I am. I did not make it, no it is making me. It is the very truth of God and not the invention of any man." What we believe, Rich is saying, makes us who we are, so we ought to be careful about what we believe. He chose to believe in the ancient truths found in the creed, and they in turn made him who he was.

The church has been entrusted with the mystery of the faith. It is a mystery because what the church proclaims is not easily understood or accepted by the world and, in fact, is a difficult set of beliefs for the world to understand. The job of the church, said the apostle Paul, is "to make everyone see what is the plan of the mystery hidden for ages in God who created all things; so that through the church the wisdom of God in its rich variety might now be made known to the rulers and authorities in the heavenly places" (Eph. 3:9–10).

God chooses to make His ways known through the church. In this sense, the church, like the incarnation of Jesus, is a divine-human enterprise. It is divine in that it is eternal and unchanging; it is human in that it is bestowed upon and proclaimed by men and women and children. It is eternal, and yet it is confined to the work of mortals. As C. S. Lewis said, "The Church will outlive the

When I first became a Christian, about fourteen years ago, I thought that I could do it on my own, by retiring to my room and reading theology, and I wouldn't go to churches and Gospel Halls; . . . I disliked very much their hymns, which I considered to be fifth-rate poems set to sixth-rate music. But as I went on I saw the great merit of it. I came up against different people of quite different outlooks and different education, and then gradually my conceit just began peeling off. I realized that the hymns (which were just sixth-rate music) were, nonetheless, being sung with devotion and benefit by an old saint in elastic-side boots in the opposite pew, and then you realize that you aren't fit to clean those boots. It gets you out of your solitary conceit.

— C. S. Lewis

universe; in it the individual person will outlive the universe. Everything that is joined to the immortal Head will share His immortality. . . . As mere biological entities, . . . we are of no account. But as organs in the Body of Christ, as stones and pillars in the temple, we are assured of our eternal self-identity and shall live to remember the galaxies as an old tale."[9]

Rich wanted to attach himself to something that would outlive the universe, and in uniting himself with the church, he became the kind of thing that will never die, an unceasing spiritual being with an eternal destiny in

God's great universe. Rich now rules and reigns in the heavens, not because of his own virtue, but because, as Lewis said, he was "joined to the immortal Head," which is Jesus.

Rich found who he was in the context of the church. He said, "When I come into church I am no longer Rich Mullins, a music education student. I am no longer Rich Mullins, a guy who grew up in Indiana. I am no longer Rich Mullins, a guy who has a record contract. All of a sudden I am a member of the kingdom of God."[10]

Many of us base our identity on what we do, or how we look, or how much money we have. But none of these form the foundation of our true identity. When we step into the church we find out who we really are: children of God and members of the kingdom. All earthly identities fall off of us at the door. The rich are no longer rich, and the poor are no longer poor. We are all one in Christ.

Rich's Love for the Hymns of the Faith

Few people love the old hymns as much as Rich Mullins did. He learned them as a child, he knew them by heart, and he insisted on closing his concerts by having the audience sing them with him, thus turning the evening from entertainment to real worship. The hymns of the church touched him in a deep place. His friend and fellow band member in Zion, Beth Lutz, says, "When I close my eyes and think of him, I see him playing hymns on the piano. When we stopped Zion, that was what I missed the most, Rich playing old hymns." A favorite saying of his was, "The reason I love the church so much is because it is the only place men will sing."

Sam Howard, another friend and a part of Zion's ministries, remembers hymn-sings in the little church next to Rich's house in Bellsburg, Tennessee: "I would look over at Rich and I would see him crying." Eric Hauck, one of the young men Rich mentored, also says, "When we sang hymns during our devotional times, he never needed a hymnal. He knew them by heart. He told me he loved the theology of the hymns as much as the melodies."

The hymns, for Rich, were theological treatises that explained the doctrines of the faith. A hymn like "Just As I Am" is the doctrine of justification by faith set to music; "It Is Well with My Soul" tells of the absolute assurance we have in God's care for us, even in our sinfulness and suffering. The hymns spoke the truth to Rich, and he could find nothing like it in contemporary praise choruses. He wrote choruses that are now sung in many praise services. He had nothing against them, but he did not feel they contained the same theological underpinnings that he found in the hymns.

Rich said of the hymns the same thing he said of the church, altering the Chesterton line:

> **There are songs that you make and there are songs that make you. I think we sometimes forget what a great heritage we, the church, have musically and how many great songs have already been written. And when you think about the music we already have in the church, it doesn't make sense anybody would be writing these days. But I don't think you write, I don't think you preach, I don't think you do anything because people need you to do it as much as because you need to do it yourself. God sends you to do it and so you do what you can and then God uses it as He wills.**[11]

Even the classic hymns were, at one time, new and progressive. Someone wrote them because, as Rich said, they themselves needed to write them. The same is true today. We sing the older hymns because they have been proven to "make" us, to change us for the better; but we also sing the new songs, the songs written by people who have the songs in them and feel the need to bring them forth and give them as a gift to the church. As in all things—preaching, teaching, praying for others—we do what we can, and God uses it.

Rich's Love for the Bible

Rich's sister, Sharon Roberts, remembers, "From the time he could read he wanted to read the Bible." When he was six years old his family started attending the Whitewater Christian Church. The Christian church's emphasis on the authority of the Bible and the centrality of the Lord's Supper took root in Rich at an early age. He attended church camp where each year there was an event called "Stump the Staff." Sharon recalls that "if one of the kids could ask a question about the Bible that none of the staff could answer, then you stumped them, and your team got points for it. Wayne stumped them every year."

The Christian church emphasizes the authority of the Bible even over the preacher. A common slogan heard from the pulpit was, "Don't trust me, go to the Bible and find out the truth for yourself." This is perhaps why Rich was so distrustful of preachers and so insistent on studying the Bible. His

It is easy to think that the Church has a lot of different objects—education, building, missions, holding services. . . . The Church exists for nothing else but to draw men into Christ, to make them little Christs. If they are not doing that, all the cathedrals, clergy, missions, sermons, even the Bible itself, are simply a waste of time. God became Man for no other purpose. It is even doubtful, you know, whether the whole universe was created for any other purpose.

— C. S. Lewis

brother, David, comments, "He didn't like preaching much, especially black-and-white preaching. He liked thought-provoking sermons with challenging ideas, but he didn't care for sermons that made it all too simple. He thought that preaching was the least important part of the service."

For Rich, the Bible was central. In his pursuit of biblical literacy, he gained more than biblical knowledge; he gained access into the presence of God. Rich understood that the reason we read the Bible at all is not to understand God but to encounter Him. Rich once said, "I don't think you read the Bible to know truth. I think you read the Bible to find God, that we encounter him there. Paul says that the Scriptures are God's breath and I kind of go, 'Wow, so let's breathe this as deeply as possible.'"[12]

Rich's love for the Bible and his desire to live a transforming orthodoxy stayed with him throughout his life. Rich and Beaker were intrigued by Saint

Francis and attempted to form a small, semimonastic community that they called "The Kid Brothers of St. Frank." In the beginning it consisted of only Rich and Beaker. Eventually they added Mitch McVicker, a student Rich met at Friends University, and Matt Johnson, Rich's cousin who toured as a roadie. Along the way they added two more: Eric Hauck, a young man from Cincinnati, and Michael Aukofer, a music student from Friends University. Even after Beaker got married and moved to Atlanta, he remained one of the Kid Brothers. The men traveled together, formed a band, and endeavored to live out the vows of poverty, chastity, and obedience without living in a monastery.

The Bible was a central part of the Brothers's daily routine. In his final two years, Rich insisted that he and the Kid Brothers begin each day with Bible-centered reflection. Mitch McVicker relates, "If we only got a few hours of sleep, he still made us get up an hour early so we could read the Scriptures and pray. He seldom talked. Mostly we just paid attention to the words of the Bible. Toward the end I felt that it was Rich's lifeblood."

The Bible, like the church, contains the truth, which can correct our misconceptions. Rich said, "I think that we were given the Scriptures, not so that we could prove that we were right about everything—it was to humble us into realizing that God is right, and the rest of us are just guessing."[13]

He also emphasized that the Bible was not as nice and tame as many want to think it is. The Scriptures and the God they reveal are shocking, and in their ability to shock us, may help us escape our narrow views. Rich wrote:

The Bible is not a book for the faint of heart—it is a book full of all the greed and glory and violence and tenderness and sex and betrayal that befits mankind. It is not the collection of pretty little anecdotes mouthed by pious little church mice—it does not so much nibble at our shoe leather as it cuts to the heart and splits the marrow from the bone. It does not give us answers fitted to our small-minded questions, but truth that goes beyond what we even know to ask.[14]

Many of us are either unaware of the earthiness and gore found in the Bible or, when faced with it, prefer to skip ahead to more pleasant passages. Rich appreciated this dimension of the Bible because he felt it was appropriate. Real life contains greed and violence, so why shouldn't the Bible as well?

The Bible, he believed, contained something larger than Rich himself could ever convey in his music. This is why he said, "I always try to put Scripture references in the liner notes of my albums because it doesn't matter what I say. I mean, ultimately, I can only tell you about my own experience. As a musician, I don't feel like I am the proper person to give dogmas."[15]

Why We Need the Church

Mitch McVicker lived with Rich for the last two years of Rich's life. Though they spent their time building hogans on the reservation and writing music, each day Rich insisted that they go to church. There was no daily Protestant service, so they went to a local Catholic church. Mitch recalls, "He said the reason he wanted to go every day was because he wanted to be a part of the body of Christ, and you do that by interacting with other members of Christ's body."

We need the church because it contains the truth (found in the creeds), because it has the songs that teach us about the faith (found in the hymns), and because we need to hear the Word of God, which according to Romans 10, is the means of faith (found in the Bible). For some, like Rich, it also offers us the body and blood of Christ, the spiritual nourishment needed to sustain life. But there is something more we need: we need to see Christ in one another.

God works through many means to reach us (nature, books, sometimes even supernatural experiences), but His primary means is through each other. We carry Christ to one another. As Dietrich Bonhoeffer explained and Rich believed, I need the Christ that is in you, and you need the Christ that is in me. We need each other. As C. S. Lewis said, we are "carriers" of Christ, whether consciously or unconsciously.

The church is not a group of people brought together by their common interests. The church is the body of Christ, a disparate group of people who have one thing in common: we are joined to the same head, which is Jesus, and we are the members of his body. The church is the place of our nurture. When we dwell with one another, even though we may disagree, we are commingling with Christ.

Most of us choose a church based on the quality of its service, but for Rich, the most important ingredient was not the dynamism of the leaders but the devotion of the people. Eric Hauck recalls being with Rich in a worship service held in a barn only a few days before Rich died. Some friends wanted to have a gathering for praising God. They encouraged everyone who had an instrument to bring it and play. Eric recalls that because they were not professional musicians, the music sounded awful. Even those who led the singing sang out of tune.

Someone asked Eric and Rich to lead the group for the rest of the evening. Rich went up to the microphone and said, "I love to be in the church. I love to listen to people sing and play with their hearts. In my profession we worry a lot about being in tune and sounding good. But this music is the music that is the most pleasing to God because it is so real, and it comes from the hearts of the children of God."

Eric concludes, "As he said this he got choked up. It was the last time I saw Rich cry."

Rich believed that an aesthetically pleasing church could distract worshipers from what is truly important. For him, the most important aspect of being in church was the connection he felt to the community of all Christians, dead and alive. Church was an emotional experience not because of how exciting the worship was but because he felt he was communing with the saints: "And this is what liturgy offers that all the razzmatazz of our modern worship can't touch. You don't go home from church going, 'Oh, I am just moved to tears.' You go home from church going, 'Wow, I just took communion, and you know what? If Augustine were alive today he would have had it with me, and maybe he is and maybe he did.'"[16]

Jimmy Abegg, a member of the Ragamuffin band, says succinctly: "For Rich, even an hour in a bad church was better than not going at all." Rich loved the church because it gave him the truth, because it allowed him to express his faith, and because it gave him a chance to be a part of the body of Christ, which he believed gave him his true identity.

The Real Job of the Church

Even though he loved the church—perhaps because he loved the church— Rich was not shy about criticizing some of its practices. He felt that the church was too easily swayed from its main objective and wasted much of its time majoring in the minor issues. He saw churches arguing, debating doctrine, and trying hard to entertain instead of transform people. He believed that the real job of the church was to proclaim the good news and then reach a hurting world with a healing touch of love.

Because Rich's music transcended denominational boundaries, he met people from many different traditions. He would play in a Baptist church on one night and then sing for a Catholic group the next. In every denomination—and certainly between denominations—he witnessed doctrinal debates that he found debilitating. His indictment was challenging.

I think that all these doctrinal statements that all the congregations come up with over the years are basically just not very worthwhile. I don't mean to sound mean toward the people who came up with them. I understand in the past there have been many heretical movements, and we still need to maintain sound doctrine. . . . But I think our real doctrine is that doctrine that is born out in our character. I think you can profess the Apostles' Creed until Jesus returns, but if you don't love somebody you never were a Christian.[17]

While he was a proponent of orthodoxy, he believed that splitting theological hairs kept many churches from focusing on loving one another.

Rich spent a lot of time talking to the Kid Brothers about the role of the church, says Eric Hauck. "He once told us that the churches, in his view, were often fighting the wrong battles. He said, 'The churches are fighting one another over theological debates, when we should be fighting for people who can't read or don't have enough to eat.'" Rich's prophetic challenge to the church was that it focus more on caring for the poor and the disenfranchised people than on throwing doctrinal stones.

Rich also had little respect for the building of megachurches. He spent a lot of time mentoring a young woman in ministry named Sherri McCready, who had been a part of a burgeoning church. He challenged Sherri to think about the more pressing duties of the church. Sherri remembers, "He exploded my theology. He talked about how the church strains at a gnat and swallows a camel—arguing doctrine and trying to grow in numbers instead of just preaching the gospel and caring for the poor. He said many churches are trying to make the lost come into their pretty buildings instead of going out to where the people are."

In his song, "Alrightokuhhuhamen," Rich wrote:

Now the Lord said Church you better love
'Cause it's a wounded world that needs a healing touch
And He gave us a promise and He gave us a job
He'll be with us but the work is up to us

Rich saw clearly how wounded the world is, and he was grieved that many churches were more interested in caring for their own interests to the neglect of the very people Jesus called us to reach.

Another error Rich saw in many churches was the tendency to cloister. Carolyn Arends, a Christian recording artist who toured with Rich, recalls a particular incident Rich related: "He told us the story about how his church would know that the kids were going to have a drinking party on Saturday night, but instead of giving them an icy reception on Sunday morning, they put on a special breakfast for them. They said, 'You're gonna have to nurse your hangover somewhere, so you might as well be here with us.'" That experience obviously had an impact on Rich, giving him a vivid experience of what Paul meant when he said that "kindness leads us to repentance," not judgment.

> *If the world grows too worldly, it can be rebuked by the Church; but if the Church grows too worldly, it cannot be adequately rebuked for worldliness by the world.*
>
> — G. K. Chesterton

Rich was also keenly aware of how segregated the church can be. He recognized that people seldom step outside their racial or economic lines for worship. One time he was playing in a conservative and slightly upscale church. He did his sound check in his usual torn jeans and T-shirt. The pastor of the church politely asked him if he was going to change his clothes for the concert, and when Rich perceived the question to be a request, he said he would. He put on a clean, white, long-sleeved shirt, but he had no other pants but his jeans. Marita Meinerts, who helped manage that concert, said, "Because he was not accepted for who he was, his demeanor changed during that concert. He felt that people were judging him because of something as trivial as his clothes."

Rich believed that churches were not intended to be galleries for displaying pretty people who cleaned up well but hospitals for people who were broken. He spoke harsh words to churches that preached prosperity, reminding them that the church is not the society of the successful but the fellowship of the forgiven. He believed that the church was not a place to make you feel good but a place you go to find God.

Rich worried that many churches had adopted the strategy of the culture, trying to reach people with a message that was comforting and made them feel good about themselves, when in fact what they may need is a message that hurts before it heals. Gary Rowe, a pastor and Rich's longtime friend and confidante, says, "Rich really hated the whole seeker-sensitive type of church service. He loved the church and longed for it to be as God intended it to be, not how humans made it to be."

One of the great dangers the church faces, Rich felt, is capitulation to the culture, adopting its methods of reaching people. While the church must strive to speak to people in terms they can understand, cultural relevance can easily lead to compromise. In his song, "While the Nations Rage," Rich envisioned the church standing strong against the lure of the world:

> The Church of God she will not bend her knees
> To the gods of this world though they promise her peace
> She stands her ground
> Stands firm on the Rock
> Watch their walls tumble down when she lives out His love

No matter how pleasing the promises of this world, the church, he believed, must stand firm in its convictions. This is something Rich was able to do in his own life, even if it meant making people angry.

Many leaders in our churches, Rich believed, are fighting a great battle. Some labor under a hierarchy that pushes them to increase their numbers. Some do so simply out of their own pride. Rich believed that this was a travesty. Instead of trying to grow bigger churches, he said, we ought to be trying to grow bigger Christians. The crucial question is not how many people are in our seats but how many we are sending out into the world to be the presence of Christ.

Nevertheless, in the midst of all of the discouragement, he still found a reason for hope. Rich trusted in Christ's promise that nothing will destroy the church. In his powerful song, "The Just Shall Live," he wrote:

> And the Church advances on the gates of hell
> And she clings to a light that will not be quelled
> By the kingdoms of this world

Rich believed that the church is not yours and it is not mine. It is not the property of its leaders. It is God's, and therefore it will stand firm even when we compromise. It always has. It always will.

Embracing the Diversity of the Church

Rich began his life in a Quaker church, grew up in the Christian church, served in a Methodist church, and at the end of his life, frequently attended a Catholic church. He was ecumenical in the best sense of the word. Never interested in trying to reduce the beliefs and practices of the denominations until they could all agree with one another, rather, he loved each for what it uniquely offered. He remarked:

> **I have a huge respect for the Quakers as people. My only hang-up with it right now is that it's so watered down. I mean, they're just like Nazarenes that don't baptize. I always wished they'd be more "Quakerly." But I wish that about everyone. I wish Baptists would be more Baptist, and I wish Anglicans would be more Anglican. We don't all have to agree. You know, a lot of people think that the idea that there's so many denominations is disillusioning. And I just kind of go, I'm glad the Baptists can go to their own place to worship, because I'm not sure I want to do it the way they do.[18]**

Rich hated to see denominations lose what was unique and interesting about them. Each was born as a corrective, he believed, and each contained important teachings and practices that existed for a reason.

Rich also believed that the plethora of denominations proved that humans are somewhat fickle. Matt Johnson, one of the Kid Brothers, remembers Rich talking about this: "He said to me, 'It's a good thing there are so many denominations because it proves that God is in control and we are just individuals trying to figure him out.'"

Rich understood that just as the world is made up of different people who like different things and do things in different ways, so is the church. He valued the diversity of the body of Christ and admired the variety he saw in the different denominations. He affirmed what C. S. Lewis said: "One fold does not mean one pool." We are all sheep who live under one Shepherd, but we are not all thrown into one giant pool and told to be exactly alike.

> *It would be better to be of no church than to be bitter toward any.*
>
> — William Penn

Rich's sister, Sharon, remembers his first encounter with different denominations. "He learned to be ecumenical when he was playing piano for our all-county choir. We were made up of kids from several denominations, and Wayne learned then that each denomination is right in its own way; they just emphasize some things more than others." That experience helped him to learn how to affirm something in every denomination, but as he grew older, he became equally skilled at pointing out some of the weaknesses.

Singer and songwriter Billy Crockett, one of the original Ragamuffins, says, "I loved the way he so deftly crossed the borders between the doctrinal faux pas. He would be equally challenging to everybody's game. The level of conversation in his life was too lofty to spend time splitting hairs about doctrinal issues. What he was interested in was much bigger than that. What he talked about was life and death for him."

Sitting in the audience at Rich's concerts confirmed what Billy said. You got the feeling that at some moment he was going to bash the sacred cow of your denomination, and he usually did. However, by the end of the concert, he found a way to affirm what was wonderful about your heritage. Rich once remarked:

Everything that has ever happened has failed, and it will continue to fail. But I think that's because God is a jealous God. And He will not share us even with our best ideas about Him. And when Christ has

stripped away all of your "phony-baloney" kind of systematic theology, all of our lame, Protestant kind of stupidity, all of our Catholic hangups, when Christ has stripped away everything that we have invented about Him, then maybe we will encounter Him as He really is. And we will know ourselves as we really are.[19]

Each denomination, like each of us, sees God through a glass, but only dimly. Sometimes what we think we know about God must be purged in order to allow the real, alive, and not very tame God to emerge. Rich himself lived with this kind of purging all the time.

Being Faithful to Your Tradition

Above all, Rich's longtime friend, Kathy Sprinkle, notes, "He believed that whatever tradition of Christianity that you came from—Methodist, Quaker, Catholic—you should embrace the best in it and love your heritage." Rich believed that we are called to be faithful to our own tradition. Certainly there may be cases where we feel as if our denomination has drifted away from us, and there is no harm in exploring other churches where we might grow more effectively. Rich himself did that, but he believed that we ought to explore our own tradition, to learn about its heritage and beliefs, and to do our best to be faithful where we are.

Michael Aukofer, one of the Kid Brothers, recalled how Rich encouraged each of them to do this, even though they were now living and working together as a community: "He told all of us Kid Brothers to learn about our church heritage and to make a commitment to our own denominations. He loved to sing hymns, and we sang them all the time, in our devotions each day, as well as in concerts. Being a Catholic, I was unfamiliar with these Protestant hymns, but I have learned to really love them." While Rich encouraged Michael to affirm his own tradition, he also helped him to appreciate others.

A part of this idea came from Rich's cynicism about finding something better in another tradition. Sam Howard, his college friend, says, "He would always say with a smile, 'Whatever church you are in you should just stay there. They are all equally messed up.'" The pursuit of the perfect church was a waste of time, he believed. And, as the old joke goes, as soon as you joined it, it would no longer be perfect. Most of all, he wanted people to respect one another's tradition. He felt that one of the greatest tragedies of the church and one of the main reasons we have lost our witness to the world is that we fight with one another. His own denominational journey exposed him to a lot of judgment, and he learned firsthand how cruel Christians can be toward one another.

Rich's Interest in Catholicism

During the last few years of his life, Rich became more and more interested in Roman Catholicism. He was drawn to the aesthetic beauty of the cathedrals—the gold, the art, the statues—and also to the mystery of the Roman Catholic faith. Probably the largest factor in this interest was his admiration of Saint Francis of Assisi. He had little knowledge of Saint Francis until he saw *Brother Sun, Sister Moon,* a Franco Zefferelli movie that would have a huge impact on him. "When I saw the life of St. Francis in this film, I was kind of going, 'That's really what I want to do. I mean, I really do want to live in poverty, I really do want my life to mean something. I really do want to imitate Christ and live according to the rule of the Gospels.' And so . . . I guess I have tried to do that throughout my life."[20]

Though Rich was drawn to Catholicism, he had trouble with some of its teachings. He went through seven months of catechism, but in the end he chose not to convert. As he put it:

A lot of the stuff which I thought was so different between Protestants and Catholics [was] not, but at the end of going through an RCIA [Right of Christian Initiation for Adults] course, I also realized that there are some real and significant differences. I'm not sure which side of the issues I come down on. My openness to Catholicism was very scary to me because, when you grow up in a church where they don't even put up a cross, many things were foreign to me. I went to an older Protestant gentleman that I've respected for years and years, and I asked him, "When does faithfulness to Jesus call us to lay aside our biases and when does it call us to stand beside them?" His answer to me was that it is not about being Catholic or Protestant. It is about being faithful to Jesus. The issue is not about which church you go to, it is about following Jesus where He leads you.[21]

Ultimately Rich was searching for the place where he could, as he said, be "faithful to Jesus." To him, that was more important than where he worshiped.

Though he never actually joined the Catholic Church, Rich's appreciation of Catholicism has helped many Protestants see its value as well. Similarly, Rich's growing Catholic audience is being exposed to ideas and images that are deeply rooted in the evangelical, Protestant tradition. The thing that Rich was most interested in was bringing the two groups together. In his life and in his death, he did much to make that happen.

Becoming God's

Neva Mullins comments, "Though he never spoke with me about becoming Catholic, I would have been OK with it if he had joined. When we get to heaven, there won't be any denominations there." That spirit dominated Rich's thinking as well. Some Protestant fans have questioned Rich's family about his journey toward Catholicism. His sister, Debbie, found a wonderful way to answer the question: "A lot of people ask if he was becoming Catholic. I tell them he wasn't becoming anything but God's."

In order to be God's, Rich believed, we have to be connected to the church. God has created the church, given it the Scriptures, the ordinances, the hymns, the prayers, and the creeds. It alone is the place where we become united to Christ, where we share in his death and resurrection and immortality. It is not a perfect society, and it may frustrate us as much as it blesses us, but we need it. We cannot live without it. We did not make it, but it is making us.

3

The Love of God

Encountering the Reckless, Raging Fury

Here I'm tested

and made worthy

Tossed about but lifted up

In the reckless raging fury

That they call the love of God

There is one thing true of all of us: we are dying to be loved. We crave it, we search for it, and if we never find it, we die spiritually. Love is our deepest reason for existence. Rich, like all of us, longed to be loved unconditionally. He was a sinner, like all of us, who struggled to believe that God could love him. But as the creed was remaking Rich, he began to learn about mercy. God was teaching him something about His love for the weak and the broken and the sinful.

I remember one time Beaker and I were hiking on the Appalachian Trail, and he met some friends of his, so I walked into town. It was about a five-mile walk from the campsite down the trail . . . , down into town. And when I got there I went into a restaurant and I was having a steak, and this guy started talking to me and we had this great conversation. We were having a good time, and he said, "Hey look, it's dark and it's five miles up the road to your campground. Why don't I drive you up there?"

And I said, "Hey, great!"

And so we got in his car, and just as we pulled out from under the last light in that town, the guy said, "You know what, I should probably tell you that I'm gay."

And I said, "Oh! I should probably tell you that I am a Christian."

And he said, "Well, if you want out of the car. . . . "

I said, "Why?"

And he said, "Well, I'm gay and you're Christian."

I said, "It's still five miles and it's still dark."

Then he said, "I thought Christians hated gays."

I said, "That's funny, I thought Christians were supposed to love. I thought that was our first command."

He said, "Well, I thought God hated gays."

And I said, "That's really funny, because I thought God was love."

And then he asked me the big one. He said, "Do you think I will go to hell for being a gay?"

Well, I'm a good Hoosier, and I puckered up to say, "Yes, of course you'll go to hell for being gay." I got ready to say that, but when I opened up my mouth it came out, "No, of course you won't go to hell for being gay." And I thought to myself, *Oh my God, I've only been in New Hampshire for one week and I've already turned into a liberal! What am I going to tell this guy now?*

Then I said to him, "No, you won't go to hell for being gay, any more than I would go to hell for being a liar. Nobody goes to hell because of what they do. We go to hell because we reject the grace that God so longs to give to us, regardless of what we do."[1]

From Guilt to Grace

Two things happened to make this foundational concept—God's unconditional love—real for Rich. These incidents would transform his life, his music, and his ministry.

In 1989 Rich worked with a youth pastor named David Busby, who said, "There is nothing you can do to make God love you more, and nothing you can do to make God love you less." Even though Rich had heard about God's love before, something in this bold statement hit him afresh. Suddenly he understood for the first time that God's love is not based on what we do or don't do. The love God has for each of us springs from His nature because God *is* love. It is not based on our performance, on our failures, on our sins, or on our successes. God's love is a reality. God loves us. Constantly.

When Rich began to wrap his mind around this concept, it began to reshape his entire view of God—and himself. Our souls are massive, and we change slowly. It would take another key moment to move Rich from hoping it was true to actually believing it.

We practice silence [when we're driving] in the truck a lot of times so we hardly ever have a tape on or anything like that. But we don't have

any rules—you can do what you want. But Beaker put in a Brennan
Manning tape and I really didn't want to hear it because I didn't know
who Brennan was and I don't ordinarily like preaching. I went, "Argh,
great." Well, I think about five minutes into it I had to pull off the road
because I was just bawling my eyes out. I thought, *I have gone to church
ever since I was . . . wee little, probably from when I was a week old,
and this is the first sermon in my memory that is the preaching of the
good news of the gospel of Christ. He's not preaching about an issue.
He's not preaching about a theological position. He's not preaching*

> *Long before any human being saw us,*
> *we are seen by God's loving eyes.*
> *Long before anyone heard us cry or laugh,*
> *we are heard by our God who is all ears for us.*
>
> — H e n r i   N o u w e n

about anything except the good news. And I thought, *Wow, this is what I
am hungry to hear. This is what I am dying to hear.*[2]

Brennan Manning's proclamation of the gospel on that tape had a powerful effect on Rich. Later Rich and Brennan would meet and become close
friends. Rich even named his band "the Ragamuffins" after reading
Brennan's book *The Ragamuffin Gospel*.

Brennan, like David Busby, also had a saying that had an impact on Rich:
"God loves us as we are, not as we should be, for we will never be as we should
be." Those two statements about God's love (that he loves us as we are and
that there is nothing we can do to change that love) dramatically altered the
way Rich thought about God.

They also altered the direction of his music and his ministry. Gay
Quisenberry, Rich's manager from 1986 to 1997, says, "The last five years of
Rich's life, the theme of all of his concerts was the love of God. Early on he

would find a theme for every tour, something he would pray about and try to discern, and it always varied. But during the last phase every concert became focused on God's love. He told me that he thought it was something that everyone needed to hear, and not just once, but constantly. Most of all, it was something he needed to hear constantly, even if it was coming from his own mouth."

Rich needed to hear this truth spoken again and again because it takes time for a new belief to replace an old one. The messages he heard growing up were different from what Brennan was preaching. Rich heard sermons of condemnation and guilt-producing homilies, and he had believed them. They had planted themselves somewhere in his soul and formed the way he thought about God and himself—that God was an angry judge and he was nothing but a sinner destined for hell.

It is hard to love an angry God. It is also difficult to see ourselves as God's beloved children if we believe we are worthless. Rich had become familiar with the spiritual foes of fear and self-hatred. But thanks to Brennan's writing and friendship, Rich slowly but certainly drew closer to Jesus and in time discovered important truths about the love of God. The excitement surrounding this discovery propelled Rich to write one of his most beautiful songs.

The Love of God

There's a wideness in God's mercy
I cannot find in my own
And He keeps his fire burning
To melt this heart of stone
Keeps me aching with a yearning
Keeps me glad to have been caught
In the reckless raging fury
That they call the love of God

Now I've seen no band of angels
But I've heard the soldier's songs
Love hangs over them like a banner
Love within them leads me on
To the battle on the journey

And it's never gonna stop
Ever-widening their mercies
And the fury of His love

Oh the love of God
Oh the love of God
The love of God

Joy and sorrow are this ocean
And in their every ebb and flow
Now the Lord a door has opened
That all hell could never close
Here I'm tested and made worthy
Tossed about but lifted up
In the reckless raging fury
That they call the love of God

The love of God is not only something we need, Rich realized, it is the reason we were made. God *loved* us into existence. God saw us before we were born and out of His love declared that we ought to be. Everything that exists came into being by the love of God. We were made to be loved.

Each of us wants desperately to be valued. Every one of us craves to be accepted as we are. Of all of our desires (for fame, power, pleasure, etc.), our desire to be loved is the deepest. The failure to find this love comprises our deepest pain and drives us (often subconsciously) into activities that we think will help us find it.

It is said that children with rickets "scratch lime from the walls." So, too, when we do not feel loved we "scratch acceptance from the walls."[3] We will do anything to get it: climb the ladder of success, try to be funny, acquire possessions, alter our bodies, etc. If we are religious, this will often translate into becoming scrupulous. We will try to be perfect or saintly in order to find acceptance from God. Every attempt to find this acceptance in anything but God will eventually fail, and we will either have to deny the pain and try to ignore it or medicate it with a drink or a pill. But we must have it. The human soul cannot endure to be unloved.

In his song, "To Tell Them," Rich wrote,

Because there ain't nobody so bad
That the Lord can't save 'em
Ain't nobody so good that they don't need God's love
And there's one thing you've got to show them
Just one thing you've got to let them see
It don't make no difference what else that you may be wanting
The love of God is the thing they need
It's the thing they need

> ## That you may love God, let Him dwell in you and love Himself through you.
>
> — Saint
>
> A u g u s t i n e

Whatever else we may think we want, the thing we *need* is God's love. Rich knew in his own heart that his most urgent longing was to feel God's love, but he would have to reconcile the problem of his own sinfulness: "How could God love someone as sinful as me?" Actually, the love we are longing for is a love that loves not in spite of but in light of our weaknesses and failures.

We long to be loved as we are, with all of our defects known. Only then will we truly feel that we are loved. But this kind of love belongs only to God. We humans are too limited to give it. That is why finding it anywhere except in God is impossible.

Discovering God's Love

The words of David Busby and Brennan Manning were part of a long, slow process that turned Rich's understanding around. Rich came to see that God shows His love in three ways. One way we come to know God's love is through creation. Rich saw the shape of God's love in the beauty of nature and its unrelenting obedience. Many people look at a tree and see nothing but a tree. Rich looked at the trees and saw God's love for him. He felt God's love in the song of a bird, the laughter of a child, and the majesty of the mountains. The created world, which Rich adored, shouts God's love if we have the ears to hear. Rich wrote:

> I love the way the scenery changes. . . . The lay of the land and the
> things people build on it all seem to be saying "don't miss this—this is a
> one-in-a-million scene." It's in that quiet, too, that all the garbled,
> frantic feelings and thoughts begin to settle, and slowly you begin to see
> the shape of the love of God. . . . The quiet, the still, small voice of God,
> the scenery, the freedom of this helpless moment where you have no op-
> portunity to be a Martha—just this privilege to sit like Mary.[4]

Another way we become aware of God's love is in the person of Jesus. If
you asked the apostle John, who wrote extensively about the love of God, how
we know that God loves us, John would simply say, "Look at Jesus." Because
God loved the world, Scripture tells us, He sent Jesus. Jesus' whole life, and
certainly His death, was an epiphany of love, a revelation of the character of
God. Despite his doubts about God's ability to love him, Rich could never get
past the person of Jesus, who, he said in his song "All the Way to Kingdom
Come," "gave love a face and . . . gave love a name." Rich's brother, David,
recalls that Rich "always struggled with feelings of self-worth. But he found
his worthiness in Christ's death for him. If Jesus was willing to die for him,
then he must be worth something."

If you asked the apostle Paul for evidence of God's love, he would say,
"God proves his love for us in that while we still were sinners Christ died for
us" (Rom. 5:8). There can be no greater proof of God's love, and more than
that, his death was for all people, regardless of their sinfulness. Rich ex-
pounded on this idea in a concert:

> Folks, God knew you at your worst before he ever sent Christ to die
> for you. And the good news of Christianity is not that Christ came into
> the world to make good little boys and girls. Christ came into the world
> to take away those sins that you've allowed to come between you and
> God. It's sad to me to believe—to look out there and see—when you're
> driving down the road and you see people who are afraid, you see people
> who are angry, and you go, "If only you knew how crazy about you God
> was! God has already loved you, if only you knew!"[5]

The third way Rich felt the love of God was through the love of other people. In fact, he said that his entire faith was constructed on the love, not the
apologetical skill, of other Christians.

I am a Christian because I have seen the love of God lived out in the lives of people who know Him. The Word has become flesh and I have encountered God in the people who have manifested (in many "unreasonable" ways) His presence—a presence that is more than convincing—it is a presence that is compelling. I am a Christian, not because someone explained the nuts and bolts of Christianity to me, but because there were people who were willing to be nuts and bolts. [6]

The love of God is incarnated—becomes manifest—in the love we experience in one another. It is God's love with skin on it.

As he grew in his understanding of God's love, Rich at times experienced it in tangible ways. His mother, Neva Mullins remembers, "He actually felt God's love. I think because he was a stranger everywhere he went, he leaned into God and drew close to Him. He was not a saint, but it was his sense of being loved by God that made him different." He certainly felt loved by his mother, a love he never doubted, a kind of anchor in the storms of his life. She gave faith hands and feet and wings.

Human love is reflection of a greater love. Just as the sun's rays are felt on our cheeks yet find their warmth in the sun itself, so do we experience God's love from others but only in a secondary way. In one of his most powerful songs, "If I Stand," he wrote:

There's a love that is fiercer
Than the love between friends
More gentle than a mother's
When her baby's at her side

The love he felt from his friends, the love he felt from his mother, no doubt sustained him and gave him evidence of his heavenly Father's love, a love that is both more fierce and more gentle.

These three evidences—creation, Jesus, and the love of others—come together to form a compelling picture of the love of God. But it is not overwhelming. We are still in a position where we must believe it by faith. God woos but never coerces. We need the help of God to receive our acceptance.

Embracing God's Love

It is not enough to have sensed this love one time, to have felt a warmed heart or a fuzzy feeling for a single moment, or even two. It is something that we grow into or, more accurately, must grow in us. It takes a long time to accept it fully because there are many obstacles we must face if we are to embrace the love of God.

Comprehending the love of God was difficult for Rich, but it is no less difficult for any of the rest of us. There is no one who can understand how much and how passionately and how tenderly God loves us. There is nothing that is beyond God, but there is much that is beyond us, and grasping this love is one of them. Amy Grant, commenting on Rich's song (cowritten with Mitch McVicker and Tom Boothe), "Nothing Is Beyond You" (which she sang on *The Jesus Album*) said, "The line in this song that slayed me the first time I heard it, and slays me every time I hear it is 'I cannot explain the way that You came to love me, except to say that nothing is beyond You.'"[7]

> *God loves us not because we are lovable, but because He is love.*
>
> — C. S. Lewis

We cannot explain this kind of love because it is so foreign to us. The love that we often speak of, the one we are most familiar with, is an emotion based on something valuable in the beloved. We fall in love, and we do so because of something wonderful about the person, the dog, or the dessert. But the emotion waxes and wanes, depending on the beloved. If he or she changes, the emotions change as well. People fall in and out of this kind of love all of the time.

The idea of being loved regardless of our behavior, the notion of being accepted despite our weaknesses, and the concept of being valued in exactly the same measure day in and day out are unfamiliar. Rich spoke insightfully on how easily we are confused:

> **I think one thing that happens frequently is that we twentieth-century American people interpret love, when we read it in the Bible, . . . as being the kind of love that we see in movies or that we read in dumb novels. The love of God is most expressed in the death of Christ. . . . God loves us with an intense love. . . . He pursues us. . . . It's not *God loves you if you're***

good, it's not *God loves you if He's having a good day*. It's *God loves you desperately, passionately*—and it's a hard thing to get ahold of. . . . But I think it's time to get past the twentieth-century and get into the way things really are.[8]

> *Our courteous Lord does not want His servants to despair because they fall often and grievously; for our falling does not hinder him in loving us.*
>
> —Lady Julian of Norwich

Rich discovered that the love God has for us is not an emotion but is in fact the essence of who God is. The death of Christ is the indisputable sign—the proof, as Paul put it—that shouts to us, "God loves you! God loves you! Look at what He did for you! He died for you! What more could God have done to show you how much He loves you!"

Not only is this divine love not an emotion; it is also not something we can merit. Our world functions on a system of rewards and punishments. If we do well, we are rewarded and we feel loved. If we fail, we are punished and we feel unloved. But the love of God is not something that is contingent on what we do. It is constant. Unfortunately, many Christians are desperately trying to earn a love they already possess and are fearful of forfeiting a love they can never lose. This whole system has to be unlearned.

Jesus understood this, and therefore he told a number of parables to help us—or rather, shock us—into grasping it. He spoke of laborers who worked different hours but got the same pay, of a selfish son who took off with Dad's money and blew it only to come home to a party. Jesus welcomed harlots and ate with sinners. The rain falls on the just and the unjust, and so does the love of God, and to our understanding it all seems unfair. That is because this love is truly a love of another kind.

Perhaps the greatest hindrance to accepting God's acceptance of us is our sinfulness. Rich Mullins was well aware of the huge gap between who he wanted to be and who he was. He spoke candidly about his own failures, even from the stage.

That chasm is the cause of much of our shame. We make promises to God, and we have every intention of being pure and perfect. We are soon confronted with our limitations, and are sometimes shocked with our own depravity. Those who pursue God, and the things of God, intensely—as Rich did—will feel this pain even more sharply. Rich's close friend and coworker with Compassion International for several years, Alyssa Loukota, notes, "Rich wanted so desperately to believe that God loved him, but he often doubted it because of his sinfulness. He believed it was true of everyone else. He knew God's hand was on him, and I think it scared him, so he would run and do something sinful to prove that he wasn't worthy of God's love." But he never could prove it because it is a love not based on our actions.

Continual failures becomes the devil's playground, for in them he whispers things like, "See, you are a sham, a fake, a sinner, and God knows it. You are deluding yourself if you think he really loves you." If we pay heed to these voices of condemnation, our confidence in God's love is easily destroyed.

Our continual falling and failing makes it difficult to believe that somehow God thinks well of us. Over time, through his friendship with Brennan Manning, Bible study, and meditation, Rich slowly grasped the truth that God is bigger than our sinfulness and is able to love us even in our darkest moments. Rich became more and more vocal about it, once writing:

Anytime that we focus on our performance, that in itself cuts us off from God—not successfully—because God's grace is greater than even our darkest sin. This is not about your righteousness. Your righteousness is all in Jesus. So don't get so hung up about how important you are in the Kingdom of God or how important you are to the growth of the church. It seems that God is always saying, "I'm not worried so much about how you're doing as much as I'm glad about who you are." The Scripture also says don't get too hung up in your failures, your weaknesses, or your addictions—it doesn't make you separate from God because he still loves you.[9]

The Death of Pride

When Rich wrote this, it was clear that he had let go of the need to earn God's love, and that in itself was a kind of death. We like to earn things. It is far more exhilarating to think that our fine performance has merited God's favorable posture toward us than it is to admit, "I am weak, broken, and there is nothing in me that demands or deserves to be loved. But I am loved nonetheless." Yet the latter attitude is precisely where Jesus said we ought to be. Coming to this place of humble confession will require that we be broken. The love of God is not only comforting but also painful in that it requires that we die to our need to feel worthy, which is in direct contrast to the spirit of the age, which tells us that we must feel good about ourselves in order to find peace. Rich often said that this is a losing effort, for whatever we think might make us feel good about ourselves (good looks, talent, wealth, intelligence) was always subject to change and could be taken from us in an instant. In one of his most poignant statements, Rich defended the line in the song, "The Love of God," that made people uncomfortable. He said:

> **I think one of the hardest things in the Christian life is (and especially for people who have grown up in America) . . . [that] we're very arrogant people. And I think it's very hard to allow God to break us. . . . Whom the Lord loves He chastens, and . . . if we'll never be broken, we'll never be saved. God doesn't break us because He hates us or because He's angry at us, but we have to be broken just like you have to break a horse.**
>
> **I know a lot of people have said, "Well, why do you say 'the reckless raging fury that they call the love of God'?" And all I can answer is, if you've ever known the love of God, you know it's nothing but reckless and it's nothing but raging. Being loved by God is one of the most painful things in the world, it's also the only thing that can bring us salvation.**[10]

Singer and songwriter Gary Chapman felt a kinship with Rich in this journey into God's mercy. "Rich spoke from such a place of confession and need and a joyful awareness of that need. He was happy to have found out that he was worthless. That is the best place in the world to be spiritually." In a similar vein, longtime friend Kathy Sprinkle said, "Rich understood that to experience the love of God, you must come to grips with your unworthiness to receive that love."

Coming to this realization is not easy, but it is the believer's destiny, a journey from falsehood into truth. It is to be aware that what God wants from us the most is not our virtues but our hearts. Rich said it this way to one audience: "Let me tell you this—God will never give up on you. He will never stop loving you. That love is a reality no matter what you do or don't do. God does not call us to be angels; He calls us to be His, and to be who we are in Him."[11]

God calls us to be His, and that means that we must learn to accept his love on His terms. As William Blake, the great romantic poet, once wrote, "We are put on this earth a little space that we may learn to bear the beams of love."[12] Rich realized that we are here to learn how to be loved, even if it is painful.

The love God has for us is not a sappy, sweet love, but an earthy, real, blood-and-guts kind of love that is willing to die for us. Rich once said, "Jesus' message is not to be good boys and girls so that when you die you can go to heaven. The message of Jesus is 'I love you. I love you so deeply it kills me.'"[13] In a column he wrote for *Release* magazine, he asked:

Could it be that God "feels"? Could God be capable of passion? Could God be excited or must He be austere? Are we comfortable with the image of God as Father and nervous about God as Lover (some of us even prefer God as Parent—less a personality, more an ideal). Are we happy to have God be the Creator, but scared to think of Him as being Creative? Do we like God being an engineer, but balk at His being an artist? Does His being a logician comfort us, but His being a poet threaten us? Do we enjoy the glow of God's light but shade ourselves from the heat of His flames? Does the idea that Jesus tolerated the sinful woman's anointing of His feet and John resting his head on Jesus' breast make us squirm, so the thought that Jesus enjoyed this makes us sick? How is it that we can accept that Moses saw a bush that burned and was not consumed, yet we doubt that God can love in a rage and never cool?[14]

While a student at Friends University, Rich agreed to teach a few sessions at our Campus Fellowship Meeting. Rich selected as his topic the Song of Solomon. I remember how shocking it was to hear God being spoken of as a lover. Rich pushed us to allow ourselves to be "ravaged" by God's love. He wanted us to let go of our stale and static views of God and explore the idea that God is absolutely in love with us.

In a concert setting, he once said:

Some of us are so afraid that God's not going to look at us, so we're out there doing all sorts of things to get God to take notice. But folks,

God notices you. The fact is, He can't take his eyes off of you. However badly you think of yourself, God is crazy about you. God is in love with you. Some of us even fear that someday we'll do something so bad that He won't notice [us] anymore. Well, let me tell you, God loves us completely. And He knew us at our worst before He ever began to love us at all. And in the love of God there are no degrees, there is only love.[15]

The Messenger and His Message

Coming to grips with the idea that God is "crazy about us" is a radical step for most people, and that is precisely why Rich began preaching it so much. He had a keen sense of his audience, and he knew that many people who came to his concerts did not think that God loved them. That is why he spent the last five years of his life talking almost exclusively about God's love. He had wrestled with God's unconditional love and at times had doubted it for himself. Old, inner voices of condemnation are hard to put to death. Rich himself knew, in his clearest moments, that God really did love him, and that understanding was so powerful that he wanted the whole world to know it.

Rich knew that most of the people who came to listen to him play in concert were people like him: they wanted to serve God, and be used of God, and yet had never settled into the blessed assurance of being loved. He liked to tell a story about his own realization of this truth: "When I was in Thailand, I met this missionary. And I was talking to her and I said, 'You know, I just want the Lord to use me.' And she said, 'Well, forget it. God doesn't need you for anything. God doesn't want to use you, He wants you to love him.'"[16]

Sensing this same misunderstanding in his audiences, Rich was relentless in sharing the good news of God's love between songs. "I preach the love of God a good bit because it's a very powerful message to me," he once said. It became the focal point of his concerts because it was the focal point of his own spiritual journey. Discovering God's love gave him peace and meaning and joy, and he could not help but to share it. He said:

For me the greatest joy that I have is knowing that I do have a Father who loves me, and that He doesn't love me in a passive way. He loves me so much that He sent Christ to take away the guilt of my sin, and that it is a real thing, that it really did happen. If I will experience joy in this life, it will be when I let other people know that there is a God who loves

them, and He has taken away the sin that separates them. There is no greater joy than just that proclamation.[17]

Ragamuffin member Jimmy Abegg remembers, "Toward the end of his life he found the center of his work, which was the love of God."

Rich's message affected both audiences and the people who played in his band over the years. As his longtime friend and Zion partner, Beth Lutz,

If we know how great is the love of Jesus for us we will never be afraid to go to Him in all our poverty, all our weakness, all our spiritual wretchedness and infirmity. Indeed, when we understand the true nature of His love for us, we will prefer to come to Him poor and helpless. We can be glad of our helplessness when we really believe that His power is made perfect in our infirmity.

— T h o m a s   M e r t o n

says, "Rich put a face on grace." Her husband, Mark, was also affected: "I was never sure where I stood with God. I watched God use Rich in a powerful way, and he didn't do the things I thought you had to do to have God like you. And then I thought, *God loves Rich,* and then it dawned on me that God loved me. That was Rich's greatest gift to me."

Studio musician Phil Madeira played in Rich's band during one of his tours. Though Phil was not well acquainted with Rich's music, he joined the tour because there was something about Rich that he wanted to know better. He says, "Every night of the '94 tour, I recall Rich's statement, 'There is nothing you can do to make God love you more, and nothing you can do to make Him love you less.' Little did I know that in my own struggles a year later, these words would see me through."

Singer Ashley Cleveland who toured with Rich in 1995, says: "Rich's presentation of the gospel in between songs in his concerts helped reach my husband, Kenny, who was not a Christian. As Rich talked about the love of God, Kenny would sit out in the audience with tears in his eyes. Shortly after that tour, . . . Kenny accepted Jesus on his own."

> *The greatest honor we can give to God is to live gladly because of the knowledge of His love.*
>
> — Lady Julian of Norwich

Guitarist Billy Crockett, who played on many of Rich's albums and toured with him for a while as the opening act, noted that there was something special, almost mystical, about the way Rich communicated God's love. "When you heard him in concert, you knew the love of God was real. He became a conduit of God's love to the audience. I would walk around the room after my set and watch the audience as he talked about feeling God's breath on his face as a child, and people were glowing."

To Rich, communicating God's love was a responsibility. Though he was a fan of all kinds of music, he believed that a Christian concert should have a message: "You know what? The world is full of musicians. What the world is starving for is Christ. If I wanna just go to a concert, I'll go see [the Irish band] the Chieftains, or a symphony, or a jazz concert, or a rock concert. But if I go to a Christian concert, I want to be reminded that He is a loving God, and that He has forgiven me, and there is hope."[18]

Songwriter and Christian musician, Billy Sprague and Rich worked together many times, and Rich's impact on him was considerable. He says, "God's love was the spark where flesh was welded to Spirit. It was the driving hot point for Rich. Every time I see Billy Graham he says the same thing—God loves you. For Rich, no matter what else you say about politics or justice or obedience, it all comes back to that. Rich taught me there is a delight in the love of God in the face of all that will happen. His message was, 'At the end of the line, it will all be well.' Rich affirmed that God is good and loving without denying that the dark parts are there."

Glad to Have Been Caught

Rich had been caught in the reckless, raging fury of the love of God, and it had transformed him. He spent the last part of his life sharing that message with others with a depth and authenticity that made audiences know that what he said was true and sprang from the depths of his soul. Kid Brother and band member Eric Hauck describes it this way: "Rich was a man who knew the joy of simply being a child of an indescribable and incomprehensible God—forgiven and loved by a loving Father. This . . . brought forth tears and a deep groaning at how much he had done that God must pierce through to love him, and yet Christ still fought through it all to love him."

This was a truth that changed Rich, and through Rich, it is changing us.

4

Boy Like Me / Man Like You

Trusting in Jesus

*And if I ever
really do grow up,
Lord I want to grow up and
be just like you*

One of the things you quickly noticed if you spent any time around Rich Mullins was his love for Jesus. He was unabashedly committed to the Savior and spent his life trying to know and follow Him. But what was unique about Rich was his desire to know and love the *real* Jesus: the God who became man, the son of Joseph and Mary, the boy who impressed the teachers in the temple, the carpenter who worked with His hands, the man who could weep and laugh and resurrect.

Rich reflected in a column he wrote for *Release* magazine:

> **Jesus is the image of the invisible God. He is incomprehensible to our Western minds—as He was to Eastern ones. He came from beyond where no human mind has visited. When we try to squeeze Him into our systems of thought, He vanishes—He slips through our grasp and then reappears and (in so many words) says, "No man takes My life from Me. No man forces his will on Me. I am not yours to handle and cheapen. You are Mine to love and make holy." In Him the fullness of the Godhead dwells. In Him all things are held together. In Him we see what love is—that it originates in God and is energized by Him. And so, we thank God for all we see. For beauty and for the miracle of sight, for music and wonder of hearing, for warmth and the sense of touch. But we thank Him more for Christ, without whom we would be deaf, insensitive and blind.** [1]

The Wonder of the Incarnation

The Incarnation—God taking on the flesh of a human being—is impossible for us to understand. The fact that Jesus was God and man at the same time is a mystery beyond our comprehension. We may feel comfortable with the humanness of Jesus, the one who gets tired and angry and anxious. Or we may want to make Him less human and think of Him more as the invincible, all-knowing, miracle-working Messiah who never doubted or ate or felt. The truth is, whatever we think we know about Jesus, He is more.

Rich understood this problem: "When we try to squeeze Him into our systems of thought, He vanishes." Jesus is bigger than our ideas about Him, and He will not allow us to reduce Him to something more comprehensible. Though we often err on one side or the other, the more common error is to make him less human and more divine. For many of us, Jesus is Superman. He leaps tall buildings and stops speeding bullets. He is above the fray of human life. For a lot of Christians, He is all God and is merely hiding in a human costume.

Even if it makes us uncomfortable, there is a great danger in neglecting the humanity of Jesus, Rich believed. If Jesus was not a human being, fully and completely, Scripture emphasizes, then He is of no value to us. He had to become one of us if He is to save us.

So how could God become a person? How could the Supreme Being live in a young Jewish girl's womb? How could the one who made the heavens and the earth sit before His mom with flash cards, learning the Hebrew alphabet? This puzzled and fascinated Rich, so he and Beaker wrote a song about it.

"Boy Like Me, Man Like You" is an example of a song where we were talking about the Incarnation, and Jesus Himself—what a hard thing. Even having grown up in the church . . . that's something I still am bamboozled by. How is Jesus fully human and fully divine—fully, fully two things? How do we communicate something that is important, but something that we don't even grasp? That's how "Boy Like Me, Man Like You" was written. [2]

The voice of the song comes from Rich's perspective, and in it he is asking Jesus if His life, particularly His boyhood, was like his own. Did Jesus wrestle with a dog and lick his nose? Did he play beneath the spray of a water hose? Did the Ruler of the Universe ever engage in the silly and beautiful things of normal childhood? Rich speculated that he might have. And if he did, isn't that wonderful?

Boy Like Me/Man Like You

You was a baby like I was once, You was cryin' in the early mornin'
You was born in a stable Lord, Reid Memorial is where I was born
They wrapped You in swaddling clothes, me they dressed in baby
*   blue*
But I was twelve years old in the meeting house, listening to the old
*   men pray*
I was tryin' hard to figure out what it was that they was tryin' to say
There You were in the temple, they said You weren't old enough to
*   know the things You knew*

Did You grow up hungry did You grow up fast?
Did the little girls giggle when You walked past?
Did You wonder what it was that made them laugh?

Did they tell You stories 'bout the saints of old?
Stories about their faith?
They say stories like that make a boy grow bold, stories like that
*   make a man walk straight*

You was a boy like I was once, but was You a boy like me
I grew up around Indiana, You grew up around Galilee
And if I ever really do grow up, Lord I want to grow up and be just
*   like You*

Did You wrestle with a dog and lick his nose?
Did You play beneath the spray of a water hose?
Did You ever make angels in the winter snow?

Did You ever get scared playing hide and seek?
Did You try not to cry when You scraped Your knee?
Did You ever skip a rock across a quiet creek?

Did they tell You stories 'bout the saints of old?
Stories about their faith?
They say stories like that make a boy grow bold, stories like that
*   make a man walk straight*

And I really may just grow up and be like You someday.

The song is playful and serious at the same time. As we listen we are allowed to imagine Jesus getting scared playing hide-and-seek or skipping a rock across a creek. Can we really imagine Jesus being shy in front of the little girls in his neighborhood? Or are we more comfortable with Jesus being smarter than the scribes? The song was born in Rich's fascination with the idea of the Almighty God stooping down to play ball among us:

> **Beaker and I started talking about the whole mystery of the Incarnation . . . what it all comes down to is, what would it be like to be God Almighty, and to inspire those prophets to write all those great books, and Moses to write those books—and then to have to become a little boy and endure Hebrew school, and listen to some rabbi rattle on about something that you wrote before he was ever born? What would it be like to be Christ? I mean, did He ever play ball? Did He ever knock a window out of somebody's house and did He ever have to explain to His dad that He had to borrow twelve dollars? So, we just started talking about what a weird thing it would be to be God and then to become flesh and then we also went on and just talked about what a weird thing to be nothing and then to become flesh. That at one time we were nothing and then we got here. And wasn't it great and aren't you glad that you were born?[3]**

Once, when we were talking about this song, I told him that I loved the image of Jesus making angels in the snow. He said, "You know, I think that is one of the funniest lines I have ever written." I looked at him puzzled and said, "What's so funny about it?" He said, "Don't you get it? Jesus made the angels . . . the *real* angels." I was stunned for a moment as I thought about the One who made Michael and Gabriel flopping his hands and feet in the snow. Rich kept looking at me and laughing, and then I laughed. I got the joke. Now I smile every time I hear that line.

The Incarnation is really God's great joke, in the best sense of the word. A good joke is all about the surprise; we never see it coming. And humor is based on incongruity, about something being out of place. Cats don't wear hats, so when we see a picture of a cat with a hat on it, we smile. Women who are ninety don't have children. All Sarah could do was laugh, which is what all good jokes make us do.

The Incarnation was both a surprise and an incongruous event. Except for the cryptic words of the prophets, we could never have seen the Incarnation coming. It does seem an odd way to save the world. It is incongruous—God cannot become enfleshed, much less as a baby . . . crazier still, in a barn. The King of kings and Lord of lords is lying in a feeding trough between an ox and an ass looking on with furled brow.

> *The Eternal Being, who knows everything and who created the whole universe, became not only a man but (before that) a baby, and before that a fetus inside a woman's body. If you want to get the hang of it, think how you would like to become a slug or a crab.*
>
> — C. S. Lewis

Heaven Came Down and Kissed the Earth

The humanness of Jesus does more than shock us and make us smile; it also affirms our own humanness. There is no greater sign of the love of God than the fact He became one of us. On that night in Bethlehem, God breathed our air for the first time.[4] The abolition of death was established in His conception and birth. The old kingdoms of this world were destroyed when God became manifest in human form. Jesus, who created the world, was now renewing all of creation. Through Jesus, heaven came down and kissed the earth.

The apostle John is explicit about the humanity of Jesus. In his first epistle, he begins by telling us that he saw and touched Jesus (1 John 1:1). He was real. He was a human being just like us. The Good News is that God has become one of us, but there were some who doubted His humanness and were uncomfortable with Jesus being fully human. That is why John began his epistle by saying, in essence, "Look, we walked with Him, we looked at Him, we touched Him, and He was just like you and me." It is hard for us to accept this sometimes because it seems impossible that God would ever have to have His diaper changed or catch a cold and need His mother to care for Him. But apparently, God did.

The Jesus Rich Knew

Rich once said, "Jesus, being God, is the perfect picture of who God is. Jesus, being man, is the picture of perfect humanity. To find Him, to meditate on Him, is to find God and our own true selves."[5] Rich longed to find the real Jesus, to study His life, and in doing so, to discover his own identity.

In order to find the real Jesus, Rich had to go beyond the usual conceptions. He had studied the New Testament from his childhood and took classes in Bible and theology at Cincinnati Bible College. Yet he sensed that all of the speculation about Jesus that goes on in academia might overlook the real Jesus. His personal pursuit of the authentic Jesus was apparently successful. Rich's college friend, Gary Rowe, said, "Rich took the 'Jesus' we heard about in Bible school and talked and sang about Him in such a way that he was able to make Jesus so real that it hurt. He made Jesus real to me, not just who I wanted Jesus to be, but the real Jesus."

Wanting Jesus to fit our images and meet our expectations is not just a modern problem; it has been true in all ages. Even if we understand that Jesus is fully human, we still expect Him to behave respectably. Even Jesus' disciples had difficulty understanding that He was indeed the Messiah promised by God. Jesus just didn't act like a king. Rich noticed this as he read the Gospels and commented:

> The disciples finally begin to get a grasp that maybe God can become flesh and dwell among us, maybe God can be a man, and then they come back and not only is God a man, but he's acting like an idiot! He's hanging out with a bunch of kids. He's blessing them, you know.
>
> And you think, *How do you bless children?* Well, the best way I know is that you pick them up and you just throw them as high as you can, and you catch them right before they splatter. You get down on all fours and you run around the room and you let them ride you and you buck them off. . . . You put your mouth against their bellies and you make funny noises.
>
> Here's Jesus probably doing all this business. His disciples were humiliated! And they said, "You should not be making such a fool of Yourself!"
>
> And Jesus says, "Here, look, look, fellas. I'll call the shots here. I may be dumb, but I am God. And I'll tell you what else, if you wanna

come into My kingdom, you'll come in like one of these or you won't come in at all."[6]

Rich was intrigued by the unpredictable, earthy Jesus he saw in the Bible. His friend and fellow artist, Carolyn Arends, says, "He looked at Jesus the same way he looked at the Bible. Just as he read the Bible in a refreshing way, he also looked at Jesus in different ways than most of us. If I am not careful, I can start reading the Bible like I take my vitamins in the morning and not read it as Rich read it. He saw Jesus and the Bible as a fascinating, funny, wildly entertaining, and profound window into the world and the heart of God."

When we see Jesus, we see what God is like. He is the true image of God. The idea of Jesus throwing children up in the air or tickling them silly did not diminish Jesus' stature in Rich's eyes. If anything, it made him more accessible. We often forget that Jesus was a joyful person. He told his disciples, "I have said these things to you so that my joy may be in you, and that your joy may be complete" (John 15:11). We have no indication that his disciples responded to this by saying, "Oh no, not *His* joy! No thanks." Clearly they wanted to receive the joy that He had because they knew Him to be a man of joy.

In Rich's songs, writing, and life, his conviction that Jesus was a very real person, someone who experienced everything in human life except sin, is clear. His music reveals a Jesus many rarely consider—a man who played with children, went to dinner with prostitutes, and spent time caring for the broken, the weak, and the outcast. The Jesus Rich knew and sang about was sometimes challenging to his friends. "He caused me to think about the person of Jesus in ways I had never done before," admits Marita Meinerts, who helped organize many of Rich's tours. "I come from a conservative evangelical church, and [Rich] caused me to think about Jesus as a real person, as a little boy, for example, interacting with His parents. He had a creative way of looking at Jesus, but often [an] uncomfortable [one] for some of us—beyond the gentle shepherd to the kind of person who hangs out with the wrong crowd."

Rich invested himself in a young man named Matt Johnson, who also happened to be his second cousin. Matt had gone to a conservative Christian college and found himself discouraged in his faith. He wrote a letter to Rich, sharing his struggles, and soon after, Rich invited him to be a roadie on his next tour. Matt describes how he would listen each night as

Rich told the audiences about Jesus. This proved to have a big impact on him. "Rich was constantly challenging my image of Jesus. Jesus had been pretty one-dimensional for me, but Rich showed me Jesus as a real person." Matt later enrolled at Friends University and finished a religion degree with, in his words, "a new way of looking at Jesus."

> *"The Word became flesh," wrote John, "and dwelt among us, full of grace and truth" (John 1:14).*
> *That is what the incarnation means.*
> *It is untheological. It is unsophisticated.*
> *It is undignified. But according to Christianity, it is the way things are. . . .*
> *One of the blunders religious people are particularly fond of making is the attempt to be more spiritual than God.*
>
> — Frederick Buechner

Not only among his friends, but in his concerts as well, Rich urged people to go beyond their stereotypes of who Jesus is. Band member Jimmy Abegg remembers: "When Rich would speak, he would often challenge his audiences to think about the person of Jesus. He would push them to ask, 'Which Jesus do you believe in—the Jesus of the right wing? The culturally acceptable Jesus who is a nice teacher? The New Age Jesus who is your buddy? Or maybe the left-wing Jesus who was an activist for your causes?' For Rich, Jesus was a real, complete, whole person with whom we are called to enter into a relationship. Rich was disappointed with people who liked some side of Jesus that fit their tastes and disregarded the rest of who he was."

The Jesus Record

Rich's desire for the world to see the real Jesus came to fruition in one of his most ambitious projects, something he referred to as *The Jesus Record*. It was to contain ten songs about Jesus. He said it was a record the Christian world needed because, for too many of us, Jesus had become domesticated, ordinary, and predictable. He wanted the album to stir people's thoughts as well as to comfort and heal them.

Unfortunately, it was a project Rich would not fully complete. He died shortly after signing a contract for the album and never got to make a polished recording. But Rich had written nine of the ten songs and recorded them on a tape recorder, sitting by himself in an old church. Thanks to modern technology, the tape was restored and the songs transferred to a compact disc, and the Ragamuffin Band and some of Rich's friends in the music industry produced a studio version of the songs as well.

The Jesus of *The Jesus Record* is one who comes as a mighty deliverer of the poor and the oppressed, a disturber of the peace, a strong lover who cuts through our pain and darkness, a homeless man who walked on water and calmed the sea, a miracle man with holes in His hands, a man who played with children and baffled the scholars, a God-man who now lives in radiance but once was let down by His friends, and finally, a man who now rules and reigns in the heavens, where He has gone to prepare a place for us.

Rich wanted us to look through that window with him because he believed we would see the fullness of Jesus, who is none other than the Jesus we need. The Bible tells us that God loved the world and therefore sent us Jesus, His only begotten Son, that through Him we might receive everlasting life (John 3:16). Jesus said He came that we might have this life, and have it abundantly (John 10:10). Our greatest need is to have this life.

Rich wanted to connect people to Jesus because He alone possesses this life. Often we miss this point and reduce Jesus to someone who can manage our sins. Rich told a story about a time when this became obvious to him:

I was at a citywide youth rally, and one of the pastors at a meeting said, "We need to tell these kids about Jesus so that they'll stop getting pregnant, stop doing drugs, and doing all these things." And I thought, "Wow, we need to tell all these kids about Jesus because Jesus wants them to know about Him. It has nothing to do with their sexual conduct

or with the management of their bodies or their minds. It has only to do with God so desperately wanting us to know that He loves us that He incarnated Himself—He became Jesus—so that we can know that."[7]

God is certainly concerned about drugs and unwanted pregnancies, but Rich believed that the root cause of all of our sin was our alienation from God. What we need, first and foremost, is to be in union with Him through Jesus, the supreme evidence of God's love. In his song, "All the Way to Kingdom Come," Rich wrote:

> We didn't know what love was 'til He came
> And He gave love a face and He gave love a name
> And He gave love away like the sky gives the rain and sun
> We were looking for heroes—He came looking for the lost
> We were searching for glory and He showed us a cross
> Now we know what love is 'cause He loves us all the way to kingdom come

The Jesus we need, Rich said, is the Jesus who shows us the love of the Father through the power of His Spirit.

If there is any meaning in the life of Jesus of Nazareth, it is this: that there is a God who created us, and who loves us so much that He would stop at nothing to bring us to Him. And I really suspect that of all the things we think we want to know, the only thing we really want to know is that we are loved. And if Jesus means anything, He means that you are loved. I hope you know that. And I hope you stop worrying about all the stuff you don't know, because I don't think it amounts to a hill of beans.[8]

He's Been There Before and He Knows What It's Like

The love of God propelled Jesus to become human and to do for us what we could never do for ourselves. Jesus lived a life that we cannot live and, in doing so, imparted His life to us. Only by being God could He defeat death, but only by being human could He suffer and die. In Jesus, who is both God and man, death has been defeated. God did not need to suffer and die, and in fact, it is not in His nature. God could never have died unless He became human.

More than dying for us, Jesus also gives His life to us—a complete human life. In order to do that, He had to become one of us, like us in every way. God could have become a tough, stoic, unfeeling kind of man, like our Hollywood idols. Instead, He became a man who wept, a man who felt everything we could ever feel: loneliness, betrayal, and fear. Again, sometimes we are reluctant to think of Jesus as lonely. But, as my colleague, Chris Kettler notes, "Because Christ became lonely, when we become lonely we are no longer lonely alone."[9] Jesus faced all that the weakest of us faces, and because of that, we have a God who understands all that we experience. We need not only the victory won in the death of Christ; we also need the completion and wholeness found in the life of Christ.

As Rich wrote in his beautiful song, "Bound to Come Some Trouble," there will be pain in our lives to be sure, but we can "reach out to Jesus and hold on tight" because, "He's been there before and He knows what it's like. You'll find He's there." We need a God who understands, a God who has lived the life we cannot live, because in doing so He enables us to share in His victory.

His Love Makes Us Beautiful

Coming into union with God through Jesus transforms us. We become different. We become better. We begin to see the world differently. Rich wrote of Jesus:

His attention and affection [were] not won by the attractive and the beautiful—His glance and His love made things and people attractive and beautiful. The touch of His hand would give sight to the blind and from the hem of His garment flowed healing. And even if someone would (and why should they) doubt the accounts of His miracles, I can testify myself I had never seen a lily until He showed me one. I had never heard a sparrow until His voice unplugged my ears. I had never known love until I met Him . . . and He is love.[10]

Jesus does not require that we become holy and perfect before we come to him. He demands that we know that we are sick and in need of a physician. When we reach out to Jesus—who has already reached out to us—we become whole and beautiful. And so does the world around us. We are all spiritually blind, and Jesus restores our vision so that we can see the world as it truly is, just as He did for Rich, who had never really seen a lily until Jesus showed him one.

Jesus desires to make us whole, to restore us to our true selves. He not only gives us His vision, He also imparts His virtue. He calmed a stormy sea, but he can also quiet an angry soul. Rich's friend Mitch McVicker, who lived with Rich on the reservation during the last two years of Rich's life, tells of a time he witnessed Rich struggling to let Jesus transform him: "When we were building the hogans down on the reservation, there were a lot of setbacks, like the days that it rained. Sometimes Rich would get really frustrated. But he said to me one day, 'It's more important to Jesus that I learn how to be patient than [that] I learn how to be a carpenter. Jesus is more interested in building my soul than He is about me building this hogan.'"

A Bold Witness

Because of his personal connection to Jesus, the one constructing his soul, Rich knew firsthand how good and loving and powerful He is. This is why Rich was never shy in telling people about Jesus—he believed that Jesus alone could save and transform people. After all, if the Incarnation is true, it is the greatest event in all of history, the focal point of everything in the universe. Rich believed that it was, in fact, true, and wondered why so many Christians shied away from telling others about Jesus. His assessment is accurate. Many of us are more eager to tell others about our new vacuum cleaner than we are to tell people about Jesus.

"Rich was very devoted to the name *Jesus*," said Sherri McCready, a fellow musician and friend, "when many others in CCM [contemporary Christian music] were shying away from it. He knew that Jesus was the only name and the only hope for the world. He felt that all of his music was, in some way, supposed to lift up Jesus."

Sam Howard, a longtime friend from Rich's early college days, said "Rich often said, 'I didn't become a Christian because of some philosophy about life, I became a Christian because of what Jesus did.' His firm belief in Christ made him bold in his witness. He was sometimes very aggressively evangelistic about Jesus—especially with strangers."

Not only with strangers, but also with the people he felt close to: Rich wanted to work on *The Jesus Record* not only so the world could hear it but also because he believed that it would impact his band, The Ragamuffins. One of the band's members, Mark Robertson, says, "He demanded that we focus on

Jesus. Not just in terms of subject matter. He wanted this project to make us better, more faithful as a band and as individuals." Another member, Rick Elias, adds, "He knew this band well. He was a Ragamuffin too. He knew we

> *When people object . . . that if Jesus was God as well as Man, then He had an unfair advantage which deprives Him for them of all value, it seems to me as if a man struggling in the water should refuse a rope thrown to him by another who had one foot on the bank, saying, "Oh but you had an unfair advantage." It is because of his advantage that He can help.*
>
> — C . S . L e w i s

needed Jesus as much as he did. He wanted to make a record that would force us all to spend time focusing on Jesus."

If I Ever Really Do Grow Up . . .

From his earliest days Rich had a passion to know about and be like Jesus. His sister, Sharon Roberts, remembers, "He always knew a lot about Jesus. He listened carefully to the preacher and to his Sunday school teachers." Rich tried to live closely to Jesus early on in his life, wanting to follow Jesus as well as he could, to love what Jesus loved and hate what Jesus hated. His oldest sister, Debbie Garrett, remembers a time when she first noticed his passion to be like Jesus. "I was raised to be kind of a tomboy. I was the boy my dad needed to help him do the work on the farm. Wayne was this artistic, sensitive kid, and I thought I needed to toughen him up so the world wouldn't hurt him. One day I decided to take him in the backyard and push him around till he fought back, because he would never fight. I knocked him down a few times and told him to fight back. But he wouldn't. I had him pinned on the ground and I said, 'C'mon, fight me.' And he looked at me with this look of sadness and seriousness and said, 'Jesus doesn't want us to fight.' I felt guilty for a long time over that. He was right. I will never forget that moment. He was this old soul in a little body."

This desire never left Rich, even in his periods of wandering and rebellion. He believed that the Christian life consisted in committing oneself to Jesus purely out of love for Him. He noticed in his own life and in the lives of his friends how easy it is to move from loving Jesus to simply believing in a doctrine about Jesus. He described the process this way:

> *He became what we are that He might make us what He is.*
>
> — A t h a n a s i u s

Christianity is about a daily walk with this person, Jesus. The heart of Christian faith is a radical and reasonable trust and focus on Jesus, but for many of us, our focus has shifted very subtly from love for Jesus and faithfulness to Him and obedience to Him to a set of doctrines. Life and living comes from God—it comes from Jesus—not from doctrine or good morals. You can be an utterly moral person and not be alive. Jesus came that we might have life, not good morals. It's not that I'm opposed to good morals at all; it's just that sometimes I think we put the cart before the horse.[11]

Rich saw Jesus as the conduit of the life and power of God. Being attached to Jesus, or to use John's word, "abiding" in Jesus (John 15:4), connects us to this life. Adherence to a doctrine or a moral principle cannot give us life. The shift away from a daily walk with Jesus to a set of beliefs about Jesus is a common problem in the church, Rich believed.

Rich constantly pushed himself to stay focused on following the risen Christ. His friend from Ireland, Steve Stockman, says, "He was very unpredictable, but he was someone who had this very focused idea on following Jesus. He wasn't interested in following leaders or following denominations or doctrines. And in Northern Ireland, you look over your shoulder and you look around to see if you're pleasing other people. Rich only wanted to please Jesus."[12]

To believe in Jesus, for Rich, meant to do what Jesus said to do. He saw it as a great contradiction to say, "I believe in Jesus," (which every Christian says) and then in the next breath say, "But I am not interested in doing what He said to do" (which, unfortunately, many of us say, perhaps not verbally, but by our actions). Rich commented on this problem by saying:

But, you know, as a Christian, one of the big questions you always ask yourself is, "So we believe in Jesus, we believe in the teachings of the church, but what does that look like when it's lived out?" Because surely, one of the things that Jesus said that I think we often overlook is, "The person who hears my words and does them is like the wise man who built his house on the rock." He didn't say "the person who hears my words and thinks about 'em" or "whoever hears my words and agrees with it." But he said, "Whoever hears it and does it."[13]

We are called to follow Jesus by doing what He said to do, and we do so because we believe that Jesus is also God. Therefore, He is not merely nice—He is brilliant and life-giving, and so are the words He gave us.

It's Hard to Be Like Jesus

The actual doing, however, is never easy. Jesus tells us to turn the other cheek, to love our enemies, and to forgive those who have harmed us. None of this comes naturally. We have been trained to strike back, hate, and hold grudges. Rich understood the difficulty of doing what Jesus said and wrote about it in his song, "Hard":

Lord it's hard to turn the other cheek
Hard to bless when others curse you
Lord it's hard to be a man of peace
Lord it's hard, it's hard, it's hard to be like Jesus

The words of Jesus are hard for us, but they are no less true because they are difficult. Not forgiving someone, for example, may be difficult, but not doing so will harm us. We may think we are punishing someone by not forgiving them, but in reality, we are punishing ourselves by continuing to carry the pain. As Anne Lamott writes, "not forgiving someone is like drinking rat poison and then waiting for the rat to die."[14] Jesus' words have never been tried and found wanting.

Rich turned to Jesus for help because he knew that living the Christian life is not merely difficult; it is impossible without God. In his song, "Jesus," he prays,

Please teach me to walk the way You did
Because I want to walk with You

This desire led him to try new ways to follow Jesus. Mitch McVicker recalls, "One of the most memorable things . . . was [Rich's] dedication to
spending time with Jesus. One year his Lenten exercise was to stay up one
hour after he wanted to go to bed so that he could spend that time with Jesus.
The disciples, he said, couldn't stay awake with Jesus when He was praying in
the Garden of Gethsemene. Rich didn't do it to be heroic; he just wanted to
do something Jesus asked of His friends."

The way to become like Jesus is through the reading of the Gospels and
spending time in solitude and prayer. These spiritual disciplines were always
important to Rich, especially in the final years of his life. He described his
own journey:

> **The goal is not that you should become a great Bible scholar. It's not
> about mere intellectual assent to a set of doctrines. The goal is that you
> should be like Jesus—and the Scriptures can help you with that. I don't
> need to read the Bible because I'm a great saint. I read the Bible because
> I'll find God there. It's about a daily walk with this person Jesus.**[15]

Growing Up to Be Like Him

Though Rich would certainly object to being compared to Jesus because
he was acutely aware of his own failings, many of his friends attest to seeing
Christ in his life. Fellow musician, Phil Keaggy says, "Rich was like Jesus in
a number of ways. They were both nonconformists in religious society. They
both had hearts that longed for God. They both breathed new life into the Old
Testament. And they both felt that fanfare and show are unnecessary, but
what really matters is what happens in the quiet places, alone. I saw a Jesus
in him that we all desire to see."

Paul said that Christians are "the aroma of Christ" (2 Cor. 2:15), that
somehow people ought to be able to smell something of Jesus on us. Nearly
everyone who was close to Rich caught the scent of Jesus (along with a hint of
patchouli, Rich's favorite cologne).

Rich's mother, Neva, recalls, "One time I was sitting in church and a little girl in front of me said to her grandmother, 'Grandma, Jesus is here.' The

grandmother said, 'Yes, He is, dear, He's always with us when we're in church.' The little girl said, 'No, really, Grandma, He's sitting downstairs.' She went downstairs and there was Wayne, just sitting there." His long hair, dark skin, and at that moment, his beard, did make him resemble what we

> *"Whoever follows me will never walk in darkness," says the Lord. By these words Christ advises us to imitate his life and habits if we wish to be truly enlightened and free from all blindness of heart. Let our primary effort, therefore, be to study the life of Jesus Christ.*
>
> — T h o m a s à K e m p i s

imagine Jesus might have looked like. But Rich was not interested in mimicking Jesus in outward appearance; he wanted to live his life as Jesus would live it if Jesus were in his place.

More than anything, Rich wanted to share the Jesus he knew with a world that desperately needed Him. Rich strove to live like Jesus and proclaim His goodness in his concerts and in his music. Though he knew that it was hard to be like Jesus, Rich never stopped trying. For those of us who listen to his music, we can hear his prayer echoing throughout the songs: "Please teach me to walk the way that You did."

During the last six months of Rich's life, I noticed a deepening I had not seen before. His commitment to living like Christ was very focused and intense. He insisted that the Kid Brothers have daily devotions and examine their lives in light of Jesus' teachings. He knew that he had to be a model for those young men, and he took the lead in living as a dedicated disciple of Jesus. As I said at his memorial service, "I saw less of Adam and more of Christ each time I saw him during the last year."

In the end, we saw a man who really had grown up to be like Him.

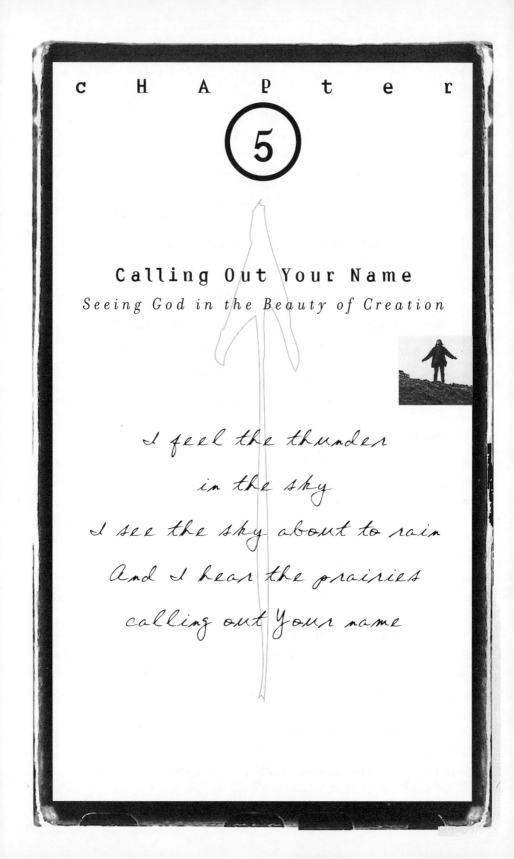

cHAPTer

5

Calling Out Your Name

Seeing God in the Beauty of Creation

*I feel the thunder
in the sky
I see the sky about to rain
And I hear the prairies
calling out Your name*

The created world inspired Rich Mullins. He loved the hills and the plains, the rivers and the mountains because they pointed him to God. He had the eyes to see the glory of God in the flowers and in the stars, and when he saw that glory, he put his pen to paper and gave us some of the most beautiful canticles of creation the world has seen since the days of St. Francis.

The prairies may look vast and silent to many, but to Rich, they were "calling out" the name of God. A lot of us drive by creeks and never think twice about them, but when Rich spent time at Johnson's Creek near his home in Tennessee, he was filled with the wonder of God's love. In fact, everywhere Rich went he saw God.

I wrote the first line of "Calling Out Your Name" when I was on [the *Unguarded*] tour with Amy Grant. . . . We were driving through Nebraska and there was a big, beautiful full moon. And I don't know how it happened, but I just thought, *Well, the moon moved past Nebraska and spoke laughter on those cold Dakota hills.* That was where it started. I went, *I will use that someday. I have no idea where but I know I will use it.* And so I just kind of stored it away. Then I was riding my motorcycle in the Flint Hills, in Kansas, and pretty much finished the song there. This would have been six years later that I finished it. But I do that. I keep little scraps. I think, writing-wise, I am probably more of a quilter than a weaver because I just get a little scrap here and a little scrap there and sew them together.[1]

God, the eternal artist, inspired Rich's artistry. He looked at a full moon hanging above Nebraska and was struck by a thought: maybe the moonlight isn't just the reflected light of the sun over those cold hills; maybe it is spreading laughter. When we hear the song, "Calling Out Your Name," we are listening to a man tell us how wonderful the created world around us truly is, and how unwise we are for neglecting to see it.

> *The world is charged with the grandeur of God.*
>
> — G e r a r d   M a n l e y   H o p k i n s

When Rich looked at something as mundane as an evening on the plains—a part of America most drivers loathe—he saw angels ascending and descending on Jacob's ladder. He saw the glory of God in a bright orange sunset. He felt the thunder of a storm and the fury in a pheasant's wings, and all of it together was calling out the name of God. As Billy Sprague said, when people listen to Rich's music, they ask, "What window is that guy looking through?" Rich looked at the world through the same eyes that Jesus did. He saw that we live in a God-bathed universe. For Rich, there was too much beauty around him for two eyes to see, but he did his best, and he wrote songs that help the rest of us catch a glimpse of what he saw.

Calling Out Your Name

Well the moon moved past Nebraska
And spilled laughter on them cold Dakota Hills
And angels danced on Jacob's stairs . . .
There is this silence in the Badlands
And over Kansas the whole universe was stilled
By the whisper of a prayer . . .
And the single hawk bursts into flight
And in the east the whole horizon is in flames

I feel the thunder in the sky
I see the sky about to rain
And I hear the prairies calling out Your name

I can feel the earth tremble
Beneath the rumbling of the buffalo hooves
And the fury in the pheasant's wings . . .
It tells me the Lord is in His temple
And there is still a faith that can make the mountains move
And a love that can make the heavens ring . . .
Where the sacred rivers meet
Beneath the shadow of the Keeper of the Plains

From the place where morning gathers,
You can look sometimes forever 'til you see
What time may never know . . .
How the Lord takes by its corners this old world
And shakes us forward—shakes us free
To run wild with the hope . . .
The hope that this thirst will not last long,
That it will soon drown
In the song not sung in vain

I know this thirst will not last long,
That it will soon drown in the song not sung in vain
I feel the thunder in the sky,
I see the sky about to rain,
And with the prairies I am calling out Your name

Creation Is Pointing to God

Having grown up on a farm, Rich was close to the natural world. He watched his dad grow innumerable plants and trees out of the Indiana clay. He spent hours on a tractor. He spent his childhood and youth getting his hands into the soil, and though he did not care for the "work" part of farming, those experiences taught him about God. Neva Mullins confirms, "Farm work teaches you about God. People in the city have no connection to the earth and how it grows everything we need. I think it would be harder to be a Christian living in the city than in the country. You can see God's order in creation, and it teaches you patience and dependence."

The psalmist says:
> The heavens declare the glory of God;
>> the skies proclaim the works of his hands.
>
> Day after day they pour forth speech;
>> night after night they display knowledge.
>
> There is no speech or language
>> where their voice is not heard.
>
> Their voice goes out into all the earth,
>> their words to the ends of the world.
>
>> (Ps. 19:1–4a, NIV)

God reveals himself to us in the created world. We see order and beauty when we look at it. It is constant and consistent, unbending and foreboding. In our scientific age we are prone to reduce the things of nature to mere physical matter that lacks any real purpose. Most of us barely take notice of the skies unless they threaten to rain on our picnic.

For Rich, the skies were speaking, day and night. For him, nature was God's tongue, and every aspect of the created world was God's speech. On the title track to his second album, "Pictures in the Sky," he sang,

> *Lord Jesus, You are the One*
> *Who made the heavens*
> *You'll take me there someday*
> *But until that time they'll hang around*
> *To say that You love me*

The clouds we fail to notice whispered to Rich that God loved him. Some people listened to his music and speculated that Rich used creation—skies and stars and moon—as a metaphor for something more spiritual. He disagreed. For him, the skies and the stars and the moon were themselves spiritual. He wrote:

> **And you might say, "but it's just a sky"—but you could say that only if you'd never seen it. And you might say, "Oh, the sky is just a metaphor and he's really overcome by something spiritual, like, say, the love of God." But if the sky is only a metaphor, it is God's metaphor, and if you'd look up—if you'd just look up . . . well, I haven't the words, but . . . There are those skies—skies stretched so tight you just know they're about to pop.[2]**

Rich wanted people to look up, to take notice, to pay attention to the homilies of the heavens and the earth, which God created before He created us. Nature is the firstborn of creation, he believed, and it has much to teach us.

The heavens and the earth were like a sacrament for Rich. By definition, a sacrament is a visible sign of an invisible grace. In the buzzing and chirping and howling of the world he heard, "God is faithful, God is good, God loves us." In an article entitled "Burning Bushes," Rich wrote, "Maybe we can hear it in the chirping of crickets or in the sound of old friends laughing . . . . Maybe the heavens do declare the glory of God, 'and the skies proclaim the works of His hands.' Maybe they themselves are His proclamation, His declaration, His sacrament. . . . I hope you see the faithfulness of God in everything He has made."³

> *In the created world around us we see the Eternal Artist, Eternal Love at work.*
>
> — E v e l y n
>
> U n d e r h i l l

Rich was in accord with Paul, who wrote, "God's invisible qualities—his eternal power and divine nature—have been clearly seen, being understood from what has been made" (Rom. 1:20, NIV). The world is a witness to God for those who will look for Him in it. For Rich, every leaf that fell was a kind of burning bush, every prairie wind contained a still small voice, and every mountain was a place of transfiguration. In the spirit of the psalmist who said to God, "You make the winds your messengers, fire and flame your ministers" (Ps. 104:4), Rich's view was that all creation is constantly pointing to God.

While living with Rich on the Navajo reservation in New Mexico, Mitch McVicker recalls, "Rich always felt so fortunate that we got to live where we did. He loved the scenery around the reservation. He was always eager to learn about nature, why this or that thing happened, like the way the plates of the earth moved and created the mountains. He was in awe of nature because he believed it was an extension of God's personality. We would go hiking almost every day, and he was always making me notice what was around us—rocks and moss and plants. He taught me to see it as God's gift. Nothing around us, he would say, is there by happenstance. It was God's handiwork."

God Invented Green

Creation showed Rich the artistry of God. He saw in the color and complexity of it all that God was a brilliant Creator. He described how a single color changed his thinking and how it led to the writing of a song:

I was thinking about how beautiful the color of green is. I was thinking something along the lines of: "Look down on this winter wheat and

> *What can be more foolish than to think that all this rare fabric of heaven and earth could come by chance, when all the skill of science is not able to make an oyster?*
>
> —Jeremy Taylor

be glad that you have made blue for the sky and the color green that fills these fields with praise." I was thinking about this old man going to Meeting and realizing on his way that he'd already been in Meeting— it's just that he hadn't been in a corporate meeting. He'd already been surrounded by the presence of God. And he looks out, and of course he's a farmer and has an appreciation for seasons, has an appreciation for that kind of thing. And all of a sudden he realizes that God invented green.[4]

Rich surmised that God must have, at some point, *invented* green. We know that when God looked upon the trees bearing fruit in the garden he looked at it and "saw that it was good" (Gen. 1:12).

This creates a whole new vision of the person of God. God is not cold, and His work is not mundane. God is burning with passion and energy and creativity. Jesus said that God does more than make the grasses in the fields; He clothes them (Matt. 6:29). He *dresses* the grass and the lilies, and no modern fashion designer can come close to matching their beauty. This is because the colors of nature are perfect. The whites and oranges and reds and blues need no alteration. Artists like Monet could only try and copy God's color scheme, but their pastels pale next to the real thing.

> *Because God created the Natural—invented it out of His love and artistry— it demands our reverence.*
>
> — C. S. Lewis

When we begin to think about the artistry of God, we come to realize that God did not create the world out of necessity. He created it that it might praise Him and lead us to Him. God created the world because of His love. In one of his most intimate pieces of writing, Rich wrote of a time he rode his motorcycle to a park at dusk and what he experienced there.

> **Right now it is dusk and far in the east the sky is already being inked with the shadow that our earth makes of itself and some nearer stars are waking there. I am in a park in Indianapolis, and right now these great trees are casting no shadows; the greens of their leaves are holding the last rays of sun already set and the sky in the west is bright and turquoise and it shines like a semi-precious stone—as if any stone could be "semi-precious."**
>
> **And over all that I can see, over my motorcycle and the trunks and limbs of these hardwood giants, over this close-cut lawn and the now abandoned tennis courts and baseball diamonds, over the sky (still fading, still and newly exquisite) and over me, a great peace washes. It comes up from the ground and down from the heavens—a deep peace breathed out by a universe that surrounds itself again to the embrace of its Creator—its God, who is to be sought by His saints in the hours of early mornings but condescends to seek out even sinners at dusk and washes them at evening in the peace of His presence and throws round their shoulders the cloak of His acceptance and puts on their fingers the ring of His pleasure—the pleasure He takes in them when He meets them**

here on the road even before they could get home, when He echoes in the evening the hymn He sang for them at dawn.[5]

For Rich, the universe was alive and breathing out a blessing to all. From dawn to dusk, God condescends to us by singing a gentle hymn through the created world. The Bible says that no human may look upon God and live, so God translates His glory into many different forms: trees and stars and rivers, animals and humans, water and sky. It is up to us to get out of our urban cocoons and take a look—which is exactly what Rich did.

> *God makes the glow worm as well as the star; the light in both is divine.*
>
> — G e o r g e   M a c D o n a l d

He loved to ride his motorcycle across the country because it helped him to feel the texture of the countryside. Gay Quisenberry says, "He was fascinated by the complexity of creation. He once told me how amazed he was that there are thirty-two different kinds of grass. That fact alone was more amazing to him than grass itself." Reunion Records executive Don Donahue recalls a time when they were driving across the country together. Don describes it this way: "He would put the music of Aaron Copland on and drive us through the countryside and say, 'Look at the pattern in that field.' I didn't care about it then, but I can tell you this: because of Rich, now I see patterns in the fields."

God Is a Joyful Being

Rich believed that God really enjoys the universe, and even more, he was certain that God desires that we enjoy it as well. He said, "The longer I live, the more I have the feeling like God looks down, like when you've just bitten into a vanilla ice cream cone, you just get the feeling God's going, 'Yes! He enjoys it, and I made his taste buds and I made vanilla and he's putting it together and he's experiencing what I created him to experience.'"[6]

We easily forget, C. S. Lewis said, that God is the author of pleasure. Too often we think that God is a fuddy-duddy when it comes to enjoying things and that the most spiritual thing we can do is go around looking sour and disappointed. *If it is fun, we think, then it must be a sin.* Rich knew better. He saw clearly that God enjoys seeing us enjoy the created world.

In a Campus Fellowship meeting at Friends University, Rich led a powerful exercise where he asked us to write down ten things we enjoyed, and anything was fair game. People put down things like sunsets and mountains but also baseball and banana splits. I remember tearing up when I wrote down, "Hearing the laughter of my son, Jacob." When I read it aloud, I noticed that Rich was smiling. Laughter was for him a great sign of grace. We ended by giving thanks to God for all of these things.

The universe is consistent, but it is not lifeless. Though the sun comes up each day, it is not a dull routine. Rich learned from G. K. Chesterton that God shouts "Yes!" to every living thing every day. God invented green. God inspires the sun. If we have the eyes to see, Rich believed, God will inspire us as well.

Rich also learned from Chesterton that the universe is not passively winding down but is energized by a God who is constantly creating and infusing it with His power. Chesterton wrote, "It is possible that God says every morning, 'Do it again' to the sun; and every evening, 'Do it again' to the moon. It may not be automatic necessity that makes all daisies alike; it may be that God makes every daisy separately but has never got tired of making them. . . . The repetition in Nature may not be a mere recurrence; it may be a theatrical encore."[7]

Everywhere I Go I See You

Rich was able, as William Blake put it:
> To see a World in a Grain of Sand
> And a Heaven in a Wild Flower
> Hold Infinity in the palm of your hand
> And Eternity in an hour[8]

Rich saw heaven in the flowers and the grasses and the trees, and he longed for every one of us to see it too. He could see heaven in the plains of Kansas and the pinions in Colorado; he could see heaven in the waves that crash up against the coast in New England or the thawing creek in Tennessee. Everywhere he went he saw God, and he was filled with the wonder of it all.

What made Rich different from many of us is that he saw God in everything. One of his most beautiful songs is an anthem to the presence of God seen in all things. In "I See You" he wrote:

Lord You're leading me
With a cloud by day
And then in the night
The glow of a burning flame
And everywhere I go I see You . . .

The eagle flies, and the rivers run
I look thru the night
And I can see the rising sun
And everywhere I go I see You . . .

In another song, "Here in America," Rich described his longing to see:

There's so much beauty around us for just two eyes to
see but everywhere I go I'm looking

> *If you think you are seeing the same show all over again seven times a week, you're crazy. Every morning you wake up to something that in all eternity never was before and never will be again. And the you that wakes up was never the same before and will never be the same again.*
>
> —Frederick Buechner

He kept his eyes wide open. His only regret was that he only had two eyes to see all of the beauty—wouldn't it be wonderful to have more eyes to see, a greater ability to take it all in? The song, "Here in America," doesn't directly mention God or Jesus, and some listeners could not understand why Rich would write this song, which described crashing waves in New England and the Appalachian Mountains. Rich responded, "There are people who think that it's a waste of space to write a song just about America—about how America is a beautiful place to live. But I think it's a waste of eyes not to notice."9

Beth Lutz says, "[Rich's] music was like a camera—he would see some beautiful place, and then it would become a lyric." Rich's song "With the Wonder" describes an area near his home in Bellsburg, Tennessee.

Down at Johnson's Creek
The trees grow tall
Like a man who feeds his soul
On Your word
And I can look in the water
I can see the stars fall
Hear the fires crackle
And the crickets chirp
And there are bluffs
On the banks of the Cumberland
Where I can see the sun rise
From a world away
And I can see the marvelous things
That You have done
In the beautiful world
That You have made

Well in the winter it's white
In the summer it's green
In the fall it's orange and red and gold
And it comes alive
In the rites of spring when the rivers thaw
And the flowers unfold
And there are beads of dew
On a spider's web
And there are motes of dust
In these beams of light
We who are bone and spittle

And muscle and sweat
We live together in a
World where
It's good to be alive

The song shows how Rich paid attention to the little things: beads of dew and motes of dust. He listened to a world that "buzzes and beeps and shimmies and shines and rattles and patters and purrs." And he was filled with the wonder of it all.

The World As Best As I Can Remember It

During a concert tour in 1989, Rich performed the same ritual every night before going onstage. He had a dry-erase board and some markers. Each night he drew a map of the earth and outlined the continents and then started filling in the countries. He would do this at a fast and furious pace until the tour manager told him it was time to go on. Then he would stop and write these words above the map: "This is the world as best as I can remember it, by Rich Mullins."

That sentence became the title of some of his finest work, *The World As Best As I Can Remember It, Volumes I and II.* Rich was fascinated by the world around him and pained by the notion that he could neither take it all in (for he only had two eyes) nor remember it as clearly as he wanted to. So he became content to remember it as best he could, and he used that exercise to help himself not to forget. The routine let him disengage from the pressure of public performance, but it also reminded him that there was a bigger world around him.

Just after he died, some of us were given a copy of one of the last things he had written, his *Goals and Resolutions for 1998.* He had written them in early September of 1997. The last was this: "Chart the movements of the Big Dipper and soak in the sun as much as possible. Live in a world that is bigger than my calendar—more permanent than my feelings, more glorious than my accomplishments (that should be easy)."

By looking up at the Big Dipper or drawing the countries in Europe and Asia, Rich connected himself with something larger and more permanent than his transient feelings and moods. Rich wanted to hold on to this perspective, and he wanted others to do the same. He had a very unique encouragement technique. When he counseled people who were depressed, he told them to walk around their neighborhoods and learn the name of every tree. Rich believed that if people could get outside of their little

> *Earth's crammed with heaven; And every common bush afire with God; But only he who sees, takes off his shoes, The rest sit round it and pluck blackberries.*
>
> — E l i z a b e t h   B a r r e t t   B r o w n i n g

shells of self-preoccupation, they could be healed of a lot of problems. They might, he surmised, see the wonder of God in the power of an oak or the beauty of a redbud. They might, just for a moment, forget their troubles (which are often self-imposed) and catch a vision of something larger and more enduring. And maybe in that simple act they would become free.

When he was caught by the beauty of some place, Rich was insistent that others go and see it. One time he made his exhausted band members stop the van and get out to look at the stars. He took the Kid Brothers to some of his favorite sights: the Redwood Forest, Canyon de Chelly, Lake Powell, the Garden of the Gods, and the Appalachian Mountains. He loved nature so much that Ragamuffin Jimmy Abegg says, "I think if it weren't for his faith in Christ, Rich could have been a pantheist."

Rich took Kid Brother Matthew Johnson to all of the sights he dearly loved. Matt remembers, "I was amazed at how he paid attention to the details. He actually had an appreciation for the moss on the rocks. He was always telling me, 'Open up your eyes, Matthew, there's a lot to see.'" Another Kid Brother, Michael Aukofer, says, "It was strange for me, at nineteen, to hear someone talk about the wind and the rain and the stars and the plains. It ended up having a real impact on me because I did not appreciate creation. . . . I do now."

Perhaps a part of Rich's secret was that he was not captive to modern gadgetry. He was blissfully ignorant of television shows. Billy Sprague, a fellow Christian recording artist who wrote with Rich, notes, "God is always trying to tell us something—always telegraphing to us, 'Notice my

> *Blessed are they who never read a newspaper,*
> *for they shall see Nature, and through her, God.*
> — H e n r y   D a v i d   T h o r e a u

presence.' Rich had his antenna on more than most of us. He didn't watch cable and 'channel surf.' He walked in the mountains. When you hitchhike, you listen. He would come back from hitchhiking with a whole batch of songs—twenty or thirty."

Canticle of the Plains

One of Rich's final projects was also his most risky, a musical he had been creating internally for several years. When it was finally released in 1997, it was a drama about Saint Francis set in post-Civil War Kansas. Rich described its plot to me: "You see, Francis—I call him Frank—comes back from the war, turns away from his father's dreams for him, shuns wealth, hears a call from God to rebuild the church, joins with a guy named Buzz (Brother Bernard), meets a woman named Claire, and heads wherever the wind takes him, totally trusting in God."

My first thought was, "Rich really needs to stick to writing songs." But as the years passed, the story became more and more intriguing. Eventually he and Beaker and Mitch McVicker wrote both the songs and script, calling it "Canticle of the Plains." Rich felt a connection to Saint Francis for several reasons, but certainly one was the Italian saint's focus on the glory of creation. Francis, who lived in the thirteenth century, composed hymns about creation that he called "The Canticle of the Sun and Moon." Rich called his musical, *Canticle of the Plains*. It is Rich's finest complete work about the glory of creation.

Created to Create

Taking the risk of writing *Canticle of the Plains* was not difficult for Rich because he was less concerned about commercial success than he was about creating something he believed in. Rich believed that the desire to create comes from God and is a duty for all Christians: "I think creativity is a very Christian thing. I think if we are created in the image of God that means we're going to have an impulse to create."[10]

The first two things God told Adam to do were to till the garden and to name the animals. We were created to create. Therefore, Rich believed, creativity is a high calling: "I think work is a very, very holy thing, and I take work very seriously. Most of us think that spiritual exercises are something you do once you get home from work, but I think what you do at your work is just as spiritual as the twenty minutes you have set aside to read Oswald Chambers."[11]

Rich disliked the notion that people work secular jobs and then do spiritual things on the side or that some people are in full-time ministry while others are in part-time ministry. He said, "If you're a plumber and you become a Christian, you don't quit being a plumber to become a preacher. You become a great plumber because your work is infused by your faith."[12] Rich believed that work was a gift from God and that all of it mattered to God. We are given the privilege of creating things because God made us the kind of creatures who need to create.

Why He Wrote Music

For Rich, the impulse to create found its outlet in music. Writing songs was his way of expressing not merely his vocation but himself. He created music because he was compelled to: "You don't write because the world needs your music; you write because you have a need to make order, to organize things. If you're a musician, you express that very human, very common need by making music. If you're a baker, you do it by making bread. It's all the same goodness, it just expresses itself in different areas."[13]

Rich made music like an apple tree makes apples. It was a natural, sometimes exuberant process, and one which he could not prevent from happening.

Playing music was always a passionate experience. As a child Rich played with so much enthusiasm that his teachers had to keep him on a tight leash. Rich's sister, Sharon Roberts, remembers, "His piano teacher, Mary Kellner, was often heard saying, 'That was nice, Richard, now play it the way it was written.' He never played it by the book. He felt more than was on the page, and he would throw himself into the song."

Beth Lutz remembers being in the practice room with Rich when he was in college in Cincinnati, watching him write songs. She recalls one afternoon: "He was really playing hard on the piano. A professor came in and shut down the piano and made him leave because he said Rich played too recklessly. Ironically, he was working on a song that would ultimately be recorded by Debby Boone and become a big hit.

Rich knew that music was his outlet, and in some ways, a kind of therapy. He said, "The thing that's cool about music is how unnecessary it is. Of all things, music is the most frivolous and the most useless. You can't eat it, you can't drive it, you can't live in it, you can't wear it. But your life wouldn't be worth much without it."[14]

Music may be unnecessary in that sense, but it is necessary to the soul. Music is love in search of sounds and words, and we need it.

Rich made music as an outlet for what was inside of him, not to become famous. Gary Chapman comments, "I don't think Rich ever thought he was supposed to be a giant success. He didn't play that game. He cared about his music, and he was proud of it, as he should be, because they were incredible creations. He wrote such different songs than anyone else did. . . . I miss them. They were unconventional. They were not cookie-cutter songs. There was not one ounce of 'fat' in them. In his songs, every word needed to be there."

Rich Mullins was not encumbered by the need to succeed; he was captive to the need to create. The difficulty in any creative activity is having the courage to reveal deep feelings to the world. Michael Aukofer learned this from watching Rich: "He said he had all of these songs inside of him, and he hoped to have the guts to bring them out. I think it was hard for him to dig so deep, and it [was] embarrassing to bring out personal struggles for the world to see. But he . . . taught me not to be afraid, and his example has really inspired me."

Because Rich dug deep, his music stands out. Singer/songwriter Michael W. Smith says succinctly, "Nobody on this planet wrote songs like he did." His music is a marvelous blend of image and sound. There is great depth lyrically, but the music is light and airy. Tai Anderson, member of the band

> *Praised be You, my Lord, with all your creatures, especially Brother Sun, who is the day and through whom You give us light. Praised be you, my Lord, through Sister Moon and the stars, for in heaven you formed them clear and precious and beautiful.*
>
> — Saint Francis of Assisi

Third Day, describes Rich's musical magic this way: "His songs have images of green pastures, of starry nights, of children at play and people in love. But as you listen, the pictures in your mind are always transformed to the face of Jesus."[15]

Rich chose to go into the music business because he felt a calling to it. He viewed a position in the music industry as a position in ministry. After several years of writing songs for other people, he wrote a letter to Jeff Mosely, then president of Reunion Records, to express his desire to become a performing artist.

> I want to be involved as much as possible in Church work. . . . I want to work in settings that are specifically designed to challenge people, to encourage people to seek their life in Christ. I would like not only to sing but to teach, . . . to "hang out" with people, to be accessible, to model faith [to] them, to be with people not as a performer, but as a practitioner of the faith. [16]

His decision to go into the music business was not to impress people, not to make a name for himself, and not to make money. He did it so that he could minister to people, and making music was the gift God had given him to use.

Like Father . . .

God's creation inspired Rich to create. For him, nature was God's art, and music was his. In Rich's writing, the two art forms blended. One night Rich wrote in his journal:

It is a beautiful night out—a good strong moon, stars, a beautiful black sky, and Wichita all lit up under it. I listened to "Adagio for

> *You cannot play the piano well unless*
> *you are singing within you.*
>
> — A r t h u r   R u b e n s t e i n

Strings" tonight. It is a beautiful sound, and . . . maybe I will some-day write something as beautiful as "Adagio," something as beauti-ful as this night. And if I had a child, I'd tell him to let these things speak to him as I cannot speak, and to see in them what cannot yet be seen in himself, and know that a day is coming when the night will envy his beauty and when "Adagio" will sound like a theory assign-ment compared to the sound that he will be—one vibrant, shimmering answer that silences the noise of proud skepticism.[17]

Clearly, while Rich heard natural wonders calling out the name of God, through nature God was also calling out to Rich. That he listened is evi-denced in his thirteen albums, countless journals, and numerous pub-lished essays and interviews. Rich was careful not only to hear God but to respond.

Spending time with Rich altered the way I look at the created world as well. Now I find myself asking, *What did I see today?* It is often very little, though I am improving. I can hear Rich asking the question this way: "Do you have any idea what you missed?" I am coming to realize just how much, but I am glad for what I have learned to see and hear. I see the color green in a new way. I hear the crickets chirp without being annoyed. And just last night the stars up in the sky were beautiful, and I thought about how Abraham looked at the same ones. And the moon—the same moon that hangs over Atlanta—looked kind of like a sliver of silver. I saw all of that after I remembered to look up, and I know whom to thank for teaching me.

6

Bound to Come Some Trouble

Growing through Struggle and Pain

I know there's bound to come

some trouble to your life

Reach out to Jesus

and hold on tight

He's been there before

and He knows what it's like

You'll find He's there

One of the teachings that Rich Mullins consistently spoke against was what some have called "the prosperity gospel." It is the belief that those who have faith in Jesus will get rich, have good health, and every circumstance of their lives will fit together in harmony. It also suggests that those who suffer tragedy, endure physical pain, and experience disappointment must lack faith. Rich heard this message preached, measured it against his own life and against the Scriptures, and found it to be false.

I think there's a big problem in the church. I think everyone thinks if you have struggles in your life it's because you're not really filled with the Holy Spirit, or you're not really reading your Bible daily, or you're doing something wrong. I think life, by nature, is a struggle. You know, whether or not you believe in the health, wealth, and prosperity doctrine, the ideas of that . . . have polluted almost all of our thinking about Christianity—where we think that a really great Christian is someone who does not struggle.

But the Apostle Paul was a man who was obviously filled with the Spirit, a man who obviously had studied the Scriptures, a man who had had an authentic encounter with the living Christ, and he prays to God and says, "Lord, I beg You to take this thorn from my flesh." Paul says, "Lord, I've been praying for You to take away this infirmity of mine, and You haven't."

And God looks down at him and *doesn't* say, "Yeah, it's because you're so spiritually immature!" God didn't look down at him and say, "Well, it's because you don't have enough faith." God didn't look at Paul and say, "Well, you know, if you would just get up earlier and pray a couple more hours in the morning" or "If you would just memorize another ten psalms." He didn't say any of that. He merely said to Paul, "Hey, My grace is plenty. My grace is sufficient."[1]

Rich cut right to the heart of the matter: "I think life, by nature, is a struggle." Life is difficult for everyone. Rich felt pain in his own life and was acutely aware of the suffering of people around him. He saw that struggles and setbacks were not always due to sinfulness but were simply a part of human existence. People get sick and die. Cars crash. Children contract diseases and never recover. Friends betray one another. Couples fight and divorce. Rich commented, "Sometimes it's hard to believe that life is good. It's not always pleasant, but life is a great gift, and your job as a human being is to go out there and live it the best you can. Christianity doesn't answer all my questions or make me comfortable and happy. What it does do is give me a context for living."[2]

> *The way of God is a daily cross. No one has ascended into heaven through an easy life.*
>
> — S a i n t   I s a a c   o f   S y r i a

Rich had a different take, an alternative way of looking at the Christian faith. Christianity was, for him, not merely a way out of his suffering, or a drug to numb his pain. The Christian faith gave him "a context for living," and part of living is suffering.

Rich once gave himself a challenge. It was a writing exercise in which he was to imagine he had a child, and he knew he was about to die. His assignment was to write down on just one page all of his best wisdom, everything he wanted to pass on to that child in his absence. Rich sat down and wrote these lyrics:

Bound to Come Some Trouble

There's bound to come some trouble to your life
But that ain't nothing to be afraid of
There's bound to come some trouble to your life
But that ain't no reason to fear

I know there's bound to come some trouble to your life
But reach out to Jesus and hold on tight
He's been there before and He knows what it's like
You'll find He's there

There's bound to come some tears up in your eyes
That ain't nothing to be ashamed of
I know there's bound to come some tears up in your eyes
That ain't no reason to fear
I know there's bound to come some tears up in your eyes
Reach out to Jesus and hold on tight
He's been there before and He knows what it's like
You'll find He's there

People say maybe things will get better
People say maybe it won't be long
And people say maybe you'll wake up tomorrow
And it'll all be gone
Well I only know that maybes just ain't enough
When you need something to hold on
There's only one thing that's clear

I know there's bound to come some trouble to your life
But that ain't nothing to be afraid of
I know there's bound to come some tears up in your eyes
That ain't no reason to fear
I know there's bound to come some trouble to your life
Reach out to Jesus and hold on tight
He's been there before and He knows what it's like
You'll find He's there

The best wisdom, the best advice Rich could give someone was this: trouble will come, but don't be afraid or ashamed; reach out to Jesus—He's been where you are—and hold on tight. The song also talks about the false wisdom others might offer: "Maybe things will get better," or "Maybe it won't last long," or "Maybe you'll wake up and your troubles will all be gone." Rich says in response to that advice: "Maybes just ain't enough when you need something to hold on to."

The one thing that was clear to Rich was that life was full of hardship. Even the most devout people undergo periods of suffering and anguish. He looked at the godly characters in the Bible and saw that all of them suffered: Joseph was left for dead by his own brothers; David hid in caves, fearing for his life; Job was covered with boils and watched as his whole world was destroyed; Jesus was whipped, beaten, and killed; Paul was thrown into prison and ultimately beheaded. The list goes on and on. Rich discovered that everyone—even the most faithful—will go through trials. He discovered this not only from the Bible; he learned it in his own life.

Personal Pain

Rich's brother, David, comments, "There was a lot of pain in Wayne's life. Our uncle died in World War II. Wayne had an engagement broken off. Our dad died. Nashville was not what he hoped it would be—it was a business more than a ministry—and his ideal was shattered. He once said to me, 'Life is hard, and it doesn't get any easier when you become a Christian.' He absolutely hated the whole 'prosperity gospel' some people preached. His approach was simply this: let people see your struggles and don't ever fake it."

Consequently, some people were surprised at Rich's candor in concerts. Rich was not afraid to share his own pain, his own fears, and even his own struggles to be faithful to God. He did this not to shock people but to help them realize that their own struggles were not a sign that God was cursing them, but rather their opportunity to reach out to God in their weakness. Rich said, "I think everyone who allows themselves to honestly be loved is going to be wounded. Your life is a gift, and out of gratitude to God you should go out there and live. And when it's all over, you're gonna be pretty wounded. And I hope that you're hurt because people have loved you, not because they have used you."[3]

What was the source of Rich's own pain? As David Mullins notes, a number of difficult events in his life. But death, heartbreak, and loss happen to most people sooner or later. According to Rich's closest friends and family, much of his pain came from the fact that he saw and felt too much. Most of us can look the other way, turn our attention to something else, and take our minds off of the cries of pain we hear around us. Rich did not have that ability. As his mother says, "He could see the pain in other [people] even before they could see it themselves."

The Burden of His Call

Rich could also see it in himself. Rich sensed his calling to minister to a hurting world. He could not escape the hand of God on his life even though this call was at times a burden for him. He once told the Kid Brothers that he saw himself as a "plow in the field that takes all of the hits as it challenges the soil." Rich felt his calling was a prophetic one in which he was to spotlight the deadly complacency of the rich and successful and comfort the wounded and broken. Eric Hauck recalls that one week Rich asked them to think about the things that prevented them from becoming who God wants them to become. "Rich then talked about how there are things that get in the way of what God is calling us to be. He said, 'My desire to be liked is the one thing that keeps me from having the courage to be that plow.'" Fortunately, he never fully gave in to the temptation to be liked and had the courage to keep speaking challenging words of truth and healing.

> God whispers to us in our pleasures, speaks to us in our conscience, but shouts in our pain; it is His megaphone to rouse a deaf world.
>
> — C. S. Lewis

Rich was not interested in merely performing for people, although he knew the temptation to please people. He often said, "Adoration is probably more addictive than any drug in the world." Rich knew that adoration was cheap and fleeting, and he wanted his music and especially his concerts to produce something lasting. He wanted to reach the hearts of those who listened. Billy Crockett recalls his tours with Rich: "I remember thinking these were rare days, and I knew they wouldn't last. Someone like that doesn't last that long in this world. Being able to so profoundly carry the paradox in his heart for so long wore him out. The stuff that is more true than the air we breathe—the love of God and the frailty of human lives—was what he lived with all of the time."

Loneliness Is a Part of Our Experience

Rich was also aware of the fact that each of us, regardless of marital status, lives with a measure of loneliness.

Even when I was engaged, even then—I had a ten-year relationship with this girl—and I would often wonder why, even in those most intimate moments of our relationship, I would still feel really

> *Do not set your heart on temporal rewards.*
> *If it were good to do so, Jesus would have thus set*
> *his heart on them. Do not fear insults,*
> *crosses and death; for if they did man harm,*
> *the humanity which God's Son assumed would*
> *not have endured them.*
>
> —Saint Augustine

lonely. And it was just a few years ago that I finally realized that friendship is not a remedy for loneliness. Loneliness is a part of our experience and if we are looking for relief from loneliness in friendship, we are only going to frustrate the friendship. Friendship, camaraderie, intimacy, all those things *and* loneliness live together in the same experience.[4]

One of his closest friends, Kathy Sprinkle, said of Rich, "Almost all of his pain revolved around his immense loneliness and his need to feel loved. As much as we loved him, we could never fill that void. I learned from him that there is within us all, if we have the guts to admit it, a terrible void created by our loneliness for God that can never be fully satisfied in this life."

The condition of loneliness was, for Rich, not a punishment but a potential blessing; not something to be avoided but a part of our lives that we should not try to escape. The sense of being alone "permeates our existence," sometimes with little noise; at other times it screams for our attention. We try to find ways to assuage the pain of alienation, but all of them fail. We seek solace in friendships, but they, too, will let us down. Rich described the plight this way:

> I think that part of being human is being alone. And being lonely. I think one of the stresses on a lot of our friendships is that we require the people we love to take away that loneliness. And they really can't. And so, when we still feel lonely, even in the company of people we love, we become angry with them because they don't do what we think they're supposed to. Which is really something that they can't do for us.[5]

> *When you are praying alone, and your spirit is dejected, and you are wearied and oppressed by your loneliness, remember then, as always, that God the Trinity looks upon you with eyes brighter than the sun.*
>
> —Saint John of Kronstadt

Rich wanted to lean into pain and learn from it. This was a determination he developed while still relatively young. Beth Lutz recalls that one evening, "We went over to Rich's apartment and something had happened . . . and he was very emotional. He was crying. He said, 'I don't want to run from the experience of the pain because I would miss what God is trying to teach me through it.' It taught me how to embrace my own pain and be grateful for the pain. And Rich knew this when he was twenty-one."

A Leveling Agent

Though Rich knew that no one could cure his loneliness and that God wanted to teach him through his pain, he also knew that it was wise to seek out support. By the late eighties, Rich had become disillusioned with the

Christian music industry and was also experiencing a lot of personal confusion. He had been taught to rely upon the counsel of an older Christian, a solid, biblically grounded person. He found such a man in Maurice Howard.

Maurice was the father of one of Rich's close friends in college, Sam Howard. Rich had met Maurice on several occasions and was impressed by his depth and maturity. Maurice worked as a counselor and pastor at Central Christian Church in Wichita, Kansas, and Rich wanted to be mentored by Maurice. He packed up and moved from Nashville to Wichita. He rented an apartment near the home of Maurice and his wife, Doris.

> *When the Ploughman ploweth deep, He expecteth a harvest.*
>
> — Samuel Rutherford

Doris describes the men's relationship this way: "Rich was free to cry with my husband and to really open up his heart to him. My husband was a rock in people's lives. He loved Rich for who he was. I think it was the stable qualities of Maurice's life that drew Rich to him. He was firm but gentle. My husband was the leveling agent in many people's lives, including Rich's."

Then the unthinkable happened. Not long after Rich moved to Wichita, Maurice died of a heart attack. The loss was devastating. Rich had grown close to the Howard family and had no other plans, so he remained in Wichita.

A few weeks after Maurice's death, Maurice's daughter, Sherri, was married, and Rich had been asked to sing at the wedding. He had written "Bound to Come Some Trouble" only a few weeks before, and he chose to sing that song at the wedding. Sam Howard recalls, "Rich almost broke down playing it." Once again, Rich's life had been visited by tragedy, and once again, he would have to find the courage to carry on.

Public Ministry, Private Pain

Over time, Rich decided to stay in Kansas—and in contemporary Christian music. His concert schedule grew busier, and many feel his songwriting took on a greater depth at this time. His manager, Gay Quisenberry, noted that something almost mystical began happening in his concerts as

The Mullins family
(l to r) Neva, John, Rich,
Sharon, Debbie
1960

Rich in 4th Grade
1966

Rich at Erlanger United
Methodist Church,
Erlanger, Kentucky
October 1976

Rich playing his first concert at Cincinnati Bible College
Fall 1974

Rich's high school graduation portrait
1974

Rich dressed up for his senior prom
1974

John and Neva Mullins
1979

Erlanger United Methodist
Church
1976

Rich at a youth group in Kingsport, Tennessee in 1978.
They gave him his first dulcimer, created by a local craftsman.

Zion - 1980 (l to r) Rich, Beth Snell Lutz, Tom Wiemer,
Jenny Filson Wesner

Rich's 25th
birthday party
October 1980

Zion
(l to r) Back Row:
Tom Weimer, Gary Rowe,
Pam Zaye Ping
Front Row: Jenny Filson,
Rich, Beth Snell Lutz
1980

Promotional poster for a coffee house in Cincinnati
Rich played so hard his fingers bled on the old piano.
December 1976

Zion at Florence Mall
1980

Rich and Beth Snell Lutz
1982

Trip to Bogota, Colombia
1988

Second trip to Colombia
1993

Rich in concert - 1987

Rich, Alyssa, and Maria Alexandria - 1993
Rich sponsored Maria from Colombia.

Smiling
1995

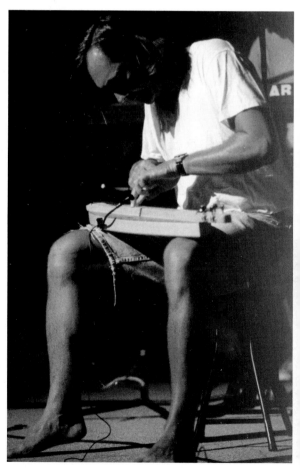

Rich in concert
1997

Navajo-style hogans built
by hand by Rich and Mitch
McVicker in 1996 in Tse
Bonito, New Mexico

Rich and Beaker in SFO
concert performing
"Step by Step."
1989

Family portrait
(l to r) Back Row: Debbie,
Rich, Lloyd, David
Front Row: Sharon, Neva,
John
1988

Rich and his mom, Neva
1992

Rich, Lynn Damon, and
April Shorty working
on the hogans
1996

Rich and Beaker in
San Francisco writing
"Boy Like Me."
Beaker learning to play th
lap dulcimer
1989

Eric Hauk, Mitch McVicker, Mark Robertson,
and Cobra Joe Curet
1997

A trip to the Grand Canyon
1997 (l to r) Matt Johnson,
Mitch McVicker, Mike
Veldhyis, Cobra Joe Curet,
Michael Aukofer,
Eric Hauk, Rich

Rehearsing for the 1997
Summer tour (l to r)
Mitch McVicker, Jordan
Richter, Rich

Rich's trailer in Tse
Bonito, New Mexico
1996

Rich and Mitch McVicker
singing
in concert
1997

Michael Aukofer, Eric Hauk,
and Mitch McVicker
Three of the Kid Brothers
of St. Frank

well. Rich was becoming a kind of conduit for the grace of God. He was speaking more honestly about his own pain and was able to reach people with his transparency. At times, Gay notes, "God spoke through Rich in ways I had never seen before or since."

At the same time, Rich was becoming aware that his own life was far from perfect. The dichotomy between his personal life and his public life became painful for him. He knew that he was not perfect, and yet he was being called to stand before audiences and give them hope and light and truth. He said later,

> I was really having a personal struggle at the time. Everyone in the band was struggling with personal stuff. I was thinking, *Man, what a goofed-up bunch of people to have to go out there. And there's, you know, a lot of people in this audience, and we're supposed to go out there and give them hope.* And I'm thinking, *You know, this is really stupid. You're calling on the wrong people. . . . I wish the people were just coming to be entertained because I don't really know what I have to give them tonight.*[6]

Rich knew that some of his audience expected him to have all of the answers, to be pure and perfect and happy. And he knew that he was none of those things. He began to doubt that God could use him, though it was clear, even to Rich, that God *was* using his words and his music to reach people. Rich knew that the source of his ministry was God, and the best he could hope for was to lead people to God and not to himself.

Afraid of the Werewolf

Throughout Rich's life, painful unrest hounded him the way Paul's thorn continually pierced the apostle. As his mom suggested, Rich's own thorn may have been his heightened self-awareness. In one of his articles, he quoted from his journal:

> Tonight, not only do I find this world frightening—I am frightened of myself. I am frightened of the evil that I am capable of. I am frightened of that which You (I believe) would deliver me from, and yet I will not let go. Help me to let go, Lord. "Deliver us from evil . . . " You taught us to pray. Maybe this fear is part of the lesson. Deliver us from evil—from

moral duplicity and weakness, from laziness and spiritual complacency, from those lies we tell ourselves from our fear of facing the truth. I think, Lord, that we're all afraid of werewolves—not afraid of being destroyed by one—afraid of being one.[7]

Rich's awareness of his own sinfulness caused him a great deal of internal anguish. Close friend Alyssa Loukota saw his struggles: "His inner turmoil was constant. It was as if a storm was always brewing inside of him. I think it was because he felt everything. As much as God was magnified in his life, so was his pain."

We all have secret desires for wealth or power or pleasure, but most of us are able to take them lightly. Rich saw them in himself and felt the need to crucify them. He wrote:

The hardest part of being a Christian is surrendering and that is where the real struggle happens. Once we have overcome our own desire to be elevated, our own desire to be recognized, our own desire to be independent and all those things that we value very much because we are Americans and we are part of this American culture—once we have overcome that struggle then God can use us as a part of His body to accomplish what the body of Christ was left here to accomplish.[8]

In many ways Rich was able to overcome the urge to be independent. He was able to face the enemy—and he found it was himself. Rich was able to surrender his life to God, and in so doing he found that God was able to use him to reach people that no one else could reach. And the medium Rich used was his music.

Into the Abyss

Music became Rich's way to deal with his struggles, but at the same time, music was also his vocation. He was torn by competing interests. On one hand he wanted to create beautiful songs that reached into the hearts of listeners and drew them closer to God. On the other hand he wanted to be a commercial success. A tragic event forced Rich to go deep within himself, and in the end he learned a valuable lesson. While working at a camp one weekend, Rich met a young man who would become a friend. As he tells the story:

About the time that my first album had totally bombed and we were starting to work on the second album, a friend of mine shot himself in the stomach. I'd been playing this song—without lyrics—for a long time, and I finally figured out what this song was about. Suddenly I realized, "This song isn't for any record, this song is for this friend of mine."

> *Wherever the will conferred by the Creator is perfectly offered back in delighted and delighting obedience by the creature, there, most undoubtedly, is heaven, and there the Holy Ghost proceeds.*
>
> C . S . L e w i s

Fortunately he wasn't very accurate about the way he shot himself, and he lived. But I thought, *I've got to say something to him*, and that's when I wrote . . . "Verge of a Miracle."[9]

Rich was searching for a way to write a song that would be a hit. But he was so touched by this young man who had lost all hope and wanted to end his life that he put together the words to a song that would become his first major hit. The irony was that he never sat down to write a popular song; he was simply writing to encourage a new friend. This taught Rich that his music should not be about pleasing people; it should be a means of helping other people see what he saw: a God who was not afraid of brokenness, a God who wanted to heal, a God who was eager to dispense miracles, a very present help in times of trouble.

Clung to a ball
That was hung in the sky
Hurled into orbit
There you are
Whether you fall down
Or whether you fly

Seems you can never get too far
Someone's waiting to put wings
Upon your flightless heart

You're on the verge of a miracle
Standing there
Oh you're on the verge of a miracle
Just waiting to be believed in
Open your eyes and see
You're on the verge of a miracle

Rich's music became a healing agent. Through the years, countless people told him how his songs carried them through times of pain. Rich's sister, Debbie, remembers, "I went to a concert and, without warning, he dedicated the song 'Verge of a Miracle' to me. I had recently gone through treatment for alcoholism, and it was his way of saying that he believed I was on the right track and that God was working a miracle in me. I played that song over and over and over after that night, and I really think it helped keep me sober through the hard times. Sometimes I didn't believe the words in that song, but it was enough that he believed it." Fellow singer Bonnie Keen of the group First Call, says, "My favorite song of Rich's is 'Bound to Come Some Trouble.' It has been a balm to me through divorce, depression, and losses of every kind over the years."[10] Amy Grant comments, "Most of us, we kind of have a brush with God, and we're enamored and frightened. But it's always kind of that barely leaning in. And Rich just had a way of running headlong into the unknown that was frightening to most of us. But in his own unique way, it seemed he always was able to find the edge and look into the abyss and come back and write a song about it and tell us what he'd seen."[11]

Broken on the Wheels of Living

Writer and speaker Brennan Manning, a very close friend to Rich, in the last years of Rich's life, describes Rich's lifelong pains this way: "There's a scene in Thornton Wilder's play, *The Angel that Troubled the Waters*, which to me really captures the essence of the life and the spirituality of Rich Mullins. The scene is a doctor who comes to the pool every day, wanting to be healed of his melancholy and his gloom and his sadness. Finally the angel appears. The doctor, he's a medical doctor, goes to step into the water. The angel blocks his entrance and says, 'No, step back, the healing is not for you.'

"The doctor pleads, 'But I've got to get into the water. I can't live this way.'

"The angel says, 'No, this moment is not for you.'

"And he says, 'But how can I live this way?'

"The angel says to him, 'Doctor, without your wounds, where would your power be? It is your melancholy that makes your low voice tremble into the hearts of men and women. The very angels themselves cannot persuade the wretched and blundering children of this earth as can one human being broken on the wheels of living. In love's service only wounded soldiers can serve.'

"And to me the theme of that story is the theme to Rich Mullins's life. All grace, all light, all truth, all power are communicated though the vulnerability, the brokenness, the utter honesty of men and women who have been shipwrecked, heartbroken, broken in the wheels of living. In love's service, only wounded soldiers can serve. And to me, the power of Rich Mullins's life lay in the power of his brokenness, the power in his unblinking honesty, his deeply moving sincerity. I miss him. But to my dying day I will . . . with honor say that Rich Mullins was my friend."[12]

Brennan captured the internal struggle Rich was facing. He wanted so badly to be free from the inner storms, but if he had, he might never have reached people. He had been broken on the wheels of life, wounded in the battle of daily existence, but it was his brokenness and woundedness that allowed him to be of service.

In all of his pain and struggle, Rich discovered God's loving hand. A friend of mine often says, "Do you know God's address? It is at the end of your rope." Rich certainly knew that to be true.

Where Is God When We Struggle?

While his music was ministering to thousands, Rich was privately crying out to God. He often felt that God answered his pleas with nothing but silence. Then an incident gave him insight into how God works in the midst of suffering. He described it this way:

I was living with Jim and Meghan Smith when I lived in Wichita, and they have a little boy named Jacob. I was sitting on the couch one day and Jacob did this thing that I loved to see—he won't do it anymore because he's too old—he used to throw these tantrums when he was two years old. He would sit on the ground and he would bang his head on the floor, throwing his arms up and down, wailing and crying. He was so dramatic! I loved that. And I would always have to go out on the porch because I would laugh and that would blow the whole thing.

One day he threw himself on the floor and was beating his head, but Meghan just stepped over him and walked into the kitchen. Man, it killed me. I didn't laugh this time. I had to leave because I was crying. And I realized, *Man, this is prophetic. Jacob is me.* I'm always throwing myself on the floor and beating my head, going, "God, if You don't give me what I want right now, I'm going to hurt Your image. I'm going to destroy the closest thing I have to You, which is me." God is not going to answer my prayer when I come to Him in a demanding way. I can beat my head until it bleeds. He can't honor that, because He is a good Father. He has to discipline [me] by saying, "Hey—I'm going to just be quiet here. I'm gonna go in the kitchen and make a pound cake."[13]

> *One sees great things from the valley; only small things from the peak.*
>
> — G. K. Chesterton

Though I was there when this happened, I had no idea that it was an epiphanal moment for Rich. He did not talk to me about it for a few weeks. I would later discover its impact on him and the insight it gave him into how we find God in the struggles of life.

Rich believed that God was somehow present to us in our deepest moments of pain but that He would not easily rescue us. Once when Saint Anthony had overcome a long period of distress, he turned to God and said, "Where were you, Lord, during this time?" He received the answer, "Nearer than ever to you." Rich never felt that God abandons us, but he believed that God allows us to struggle in order to grow.

Sanctified by Our Struggles

Rich also believed that God may even provide trying situations to help us grow. He once said, "It never fails. God will put people in your path that irritate you, especially if you're prone to be irritated."[14] Father Matt McGinnis was a close friend to Rich during the last few years of Rich's life, witnessed some of Rich's testing periods, and commented, "Rich's struggles sanctified him."

In a booklet he wrote, Rich talked about how God interacted with Joseph. Instead of giving Joseph a series of blessings, God gave him difficult circumstances:

> God did not give Joseph any special information about how to get from being the son of a nomad in Palestine to being Pharaoh's right hand man in Egypt. What He did give Joseph was eleven jealous brothers, the attention of a very loose and vengeful woman, the ability to do the service of interpreting dreams and managing other people's affairs, and the grace to do that faithfully wherever he was.[15]

Rich wrote a song called "Jacob and 2 Women" that described Jacob's hardships not only in having to care for two wives but also in feeling the pain of losing Rachel, who died giving birth to Benjamin. The story of Benjamin's naming was deeply instructive for Rich. He said:

> Rachel died giving birth to Benjamin, only her second child. So here she is dying while giving birth, and she names him Ben-o-me, which means son of my sorrows. But Jacob says, "I won't call him that, but I will call him Benjamin, which means son of my strength." As if to say to Rachel, "Your beauty is my strength. You are not just a beautiful woman, you are my strength."[16]

Rich understood the paradox that sorrow can lead to strength, that suffering can lead to growth. Though we would never ask for trying circumstances, if we are honest we will admit that those times in our lives when we struggled were our most transforming moments. Paul stated it best when he said, "Our light, momentary afflictions are preparing us for an eternal weight of glory" (2 Cor. 4:17). In light of eternity, our suffering is momentary, and it works to shape us for an eternal weight of glory.

Because he understood this, Rich learned to give thanks even for his pain. In a song he wrote with Pam Mark Hall, Mike Hudson, and Keith Thomas called "The Agony and the Glory," he said:

We give thanks for the sun
We give thanks for the rain
He is Lord of them all
All the joy and the pain

We've gotta live with the agony and the glory
Through the pain and joy
We can learn to rejoice
And embrace both sides of the story
Not a single moment goes to waste
If it works to make you holy
Let the Spirit have His way with you

Through the agony and the glory

To be sure, struggles can break people if not endured with the power of faith. But Rich looked at the pain in his life and discovered the truth of what Dante meant when he wrote, "In accepting what God wills for us do we find our peace."

Worthy to Suffer

Rich believed that suffering is actually often a sign of God's favor. He said, "Someone once asked Mother Teresa if she thought that we didn't suffer in the United States like other people did because we were a righteous nation, and Mother Teresa said, 'Oh, no, I'm afraid you're so wrong.' They said, 'What do you mean?' She said, 'I don't think you suffer because I don't think you are worthy to suffer.'" This story prompted Rich to conclude, "Don't resist the work of God by asking for an easy life."[17]

This is why James encourages us to "consider it pure joy" when we suffer through trials (James 1:2, NIV). After a painful time of heartbreak, Rich took his own counsel and tried to find a way to give God thanks.

I wrote the song "Damascus Road" right after my ex-fiancé called off our engagement, and I just sort of did it as an act of obedience.

Because the Hebrew people were required to say, "The Lord giveth, the Lord taketh away, blessed be the name of the Lord" when a tragedy happened. So I thought, *Well, you know I need to do something along those lines.* So I decided to just thank God. It was sort of a writing exercise. But by the time it was over, I realized that sometimes God has better

> *For this is also the work of the loving-kindness of God, that our struggles are not protracted to a great length, but that after struggling for a brief and tiny twinkling of an eye (for such is life compared with the other) we receive crowns of victory for endless ages.*
>
> — S a i n t   J o h n   C h r y s o s t o m

things in mind or something different in mind for us than what we have in mind for ourselves. The long and short of all of it is that if I believe that God is good, then I need to accept whatever happens to me in life as being a gift, and allow Him to take some of the things that hurt, allow Him to take some of the things that sting, some of the things that I think are going to kill me—allow Him to take those things and make of me the person He wants me to be. It may not be the person I want to be, but it'll be the person He would want me to be.[18]

The song Rich wrote (with Beaker) records lyrically his personal pivot from self-seeking to surrender:

D a m a s c u s   R o a d

On the road to Damascus
I was hung in the ropes of success
When You stripped away the mask of life
They had placed upon the face of death
And I wanna thank You Lord

More than all of my words can say
I give my life to sing your praise
All those fortunes I hoarded
They were the well from which my poverty sprang
They led me to no greater glory
And they left me with no less shame
I say I wanna give You glory Lord and I do
But everything that I could ever find to offer comes from You
But if my darkness can praise Your light
You give me breath
And I'll give my life
To sing Your praise
On the road to Damascus
I was hung in the ropes of success
When You stripped away the mask of life
They had placed upon the face of death
And I wanna thank You Lord
More than all of my words can say
I give my life to sing your praise

The issue that resulted in "Damascus Road," a broken engagement, was a concern to people who loved Rich. Many desperately wanted Rich to be happily married. While that never happened, Rich was not bitter. He believed that he had a wonderful life full of great friendships, tremendous opportunities, and God-given gifts to write and sing. Toward the end of his life he said, "Right now I cannot imagine that life could be happier married than it is single, so I'm not in a panic about getting married. And I think, you know, maybe God wanted me to be celibate and the way that He accomplished that was to break my heart. So that's the way it goes."[19]

Don't Be Afraid

Rich could say all of this because he believed that in the end those who are God's have no reason to fear what will happen to them. In the grand scheme of life, all pain and suffering will—if given to God—have served to make us better and stronger disciples. Rich's ability to see beyond the temporal concerns of this world helped him learn how not to be afraid. At a concert in 1995, he said:

Tonight I'm going to say to you what the angels said to every charac-ter in the Bible that they encountered. . . . They said, "Don't be afraid." We've got a little while to go yet in this life, and it's a scary thing, but don't be afraid. Be of good cheer. He has overcome the world. And He has chosen to dwell within us. And we ain't all that big a deal, but our Savior is. He will walk with us through this life, and when it's over, He will raise us up again and take us to be where He is. Not because of what we've done, but because of who He is. Because of the love He has for us.[20]

Rich understood that trouble was bound to come, but Jesus would be there in the midst of it. Brennan Manning, Rich's friend and spiritual direc-tor, often uses the following benediction. Nothing I know of better expresses what Rich understood about the value of struggle.

May all of your expectations be frustrated,
May all of your plans be thwarted,
May all of your desires be withered into nothingness,
That you may experience the powerlessness and poverty of a child
And can sing and dance in the love of God,
Who is Father, Son, and Holy Spirit.

7

My One Thing

Finding Freedom in Simplicity

Save me from those things
that might distract me
Please take them away
and purify my heart
I don't want to lose the eternal
for the things that are passing
'Cause what will I have
when the world is gone
If it isn't for the love
that goes on and on
with my one thing
You're my one thing

One of the most striking features about Rich Mullins was his lifestyle. Rich lived very simply. He had few possessions. He did not care about money. He had no desire for power. He wasted little energy seeking success. What he did care about, passionately, was the kingdom of heaven, and he ordered his life around its pursuit.

I really struggle with American Christianity. People in America grow up in a culture that worships pleasure, leisure, and affluence. I think the church is doubly damned when it uses Jesus as a vehicle for achieving all of that. Many people believe that if you give a tithe to the church then God will make you rich. Why? . . . If you give a tithe, you get rid of ten percent of the root of all evil. You should be giving ninety percent because God can handle money better than we can.[1]

The Freedom of Simplicity

Because he lived simply, Rich was free, and many envied this in him. Rich had discovered that when ambition lifts freedom falls like rain. There is great freedom in simplicity. If everyone were suddenly to stop desiring to have more money or fame—as Rich did—we would find ourselves free of the pressure to do more. Free to be alone with God, free to drive across the country, free to spend time with our family and friends, free to hike the Appalachian Trail. Amy Grant admired the way Rich "was free to give in to every Bohemian impulse that he ever had, the ones which most of us are unable to pursue because we live within the boundaries of our careers."

Some people looked at Rich's life and longed to imitate it, but what they failed to see is that simplicity is an *inward* disposition. It's a firm conviction that the things of this world are nice but passing, that money and fame cannot buy us happiness, that what we really need and deeply desire is to be in union with God. In fact, money and fame might actually detract us from seeking first the Kingdom of God. Trying to imitate the outer effects of simplicity without the inner disposition will lead to frustration and failure. The inner disposition then naturally leads to the outer lifestyle. As Jesus said,

> *If people would only consider how hard it is to obtain money, how uncertainly it is kept, the envy it brings, that it can neither make a man wise, nor cure diseases, nor add to life, much less give peace in death, people would not care to keep such a low and impotent thing as money.*
>
> — William Penn

"The tree is known by its fruit," which is a way of saying, "The inner determines the outer, and not vice versa" (see Matt. 7:17–18, 20).

The philosopher, Søren Kierkegaard, once wrote, "Purity of heart is to will one thing." This statement had a profound impact on Rich. He knew that the inner desires determine the outer behavior, and he longed for God to purify his heart by focusing on God's rule and reign within. He also knew that worldly treasures competed for his allegiance, and he earnestly wanted to stay focused on that "one thing." He wrote a song describing this yearning.

My One Thing

Everybody I know says they need just one thing
And what they really mean is that they need just one thing more
And everybody seems to think they got it coming
Well I know that I don't deserve You
Still I want to love and serve You more and more
You're my one thing

Save me from those things that might distract me
Please take them away and purify my heart

I don't want to lose the eternal for the things that are passing
'Cause what will I have when the world is gone
If it isn't for the love that goes on and on with

My one thing
You're my one thing
And the pure in heart shall see God . . .
Who have I in Heaven but You Jesus
And what better could I hope to find down here on earth
I could cross the most distant reaches of this world
But I'd just be wasting my time 'cause
I'm certain already I'm sure I'd find You're
My one thing
You're my one thing
And the pure in heart shall see God . . .

Every night every day
You hold on tight
Or you drift away
You're left to live
With the choices you make
Oh Lord please give me the strength
To watch and work and love and sing and pray

Who have I in Heaven but You Jesus
And what better could I hope to find down here on earth
I could cross the most distant reaches of this world
But I'd just be wasting my time 'cause
I'm certain already I'm sure I'd find You're

My one thing
You're my one thing
And the pure in heart shall see God . . .

Rich once joked about the irony of the fact that the song itself was successful even though it lacked a lot of special studio effects: "'My One Thing' was written and performed on a hammered dulcimer, and went to number one on pop Christian charts. How many hammered dulcimer songs are there—and this goes to number one. That's weird!"[2] The song is actually a prayer, asking God to save him from "the things that might distract" him.

Rich focused on the "one thing," which is Jesus and His now-available kingdom. This is not easy, especially in our culture, which is why he prays, "O Lord, please give me the strength to watch and work and love and sing and pray." He did not want "to lose the eternal for the things that are passing." Rich knew that we cannot keep treasures of this earth. Paul said it clearly: "For we brought nothing into the world, so that we can take nothing out of it" (1 Tim. 6:7).

The Origins of His Simplicity

In order to understand why Rich yearned for simplicity, why he had so few possessions, or why he chose to live in attics and trailers when he could have lived in a mansion, we have to look inside, into his soul to see what made him live this way. Rich grew up in a very nonmaterialistic family. He learned from his parents that the things that are really valuable do not cost money. Even cornbread and beans are a gourmet meal to the right palate. Also, his Quaker heritage—Quakers were known for their simplicity—played a role in the development of his lifestyle.

In his youth Rich had a deep hunger for God and a strong desire to imitate Jesus. In the Gospels he saw Jesus denounce the pursuit of wealth, saying, "Woe to them that are rich." He told the rich young ruler to sell his possessions and give the money to the poor, saying that the rich had as much chance getting into heaven as a camel had of going through the eye of a needle. And Jesus called money a rival god, saying that people could not be faithful to God and money at the same time.

As a young man Rich wanted to obey Jesus above all else, and when he saw Jesus' example, he began to view money and possessions as potentially dangerous. Neva Mullins says, "He always had a hard time with money. . . . I think he was afraid of what money can do to people, and he didn't want it to happen to him."

As Rich grew older, this attitude only intensified. While in college in Cincinnati he lived near the poverty line. His mother recalls, "One time when he was going back to college, I asked him if he had any money. He said,

'Yes.' I said, 'Show me.' He reached in his pockets and pulled out a handful of change. His dad had filled his tank with gas, so he figured that a pocketful of change was enough to get himself to Cincinnati, and that was all he needed."

While in college, Rich worked part-time in a parking garage to help pay for school. He refused to receive money from his parents. Friend Kathy Sprinkle remembers, "In college he was so poor that he used to go to the local pizza parlor and just order a Coke and wait until people would leave. He would then take their half-eaten pieces of pizza and eat them. Also, he would pad his hamburgers at fast-food restaurants with several packages of crackers. He said he did this in order to fill himself up for less money."

> *To be clever enough to get a great deal of money, one must be stupid enough to want it.*
>
> — G. K. Chesterton

When we hear such stories, we may feel sorry for Rich. But in reality, he would tell you that he was not unhappy because he lacked money, or that he would have been happier if he had more. He learned from an early age this fundamental truth: money and possessions will not make us happy. The rest of us are simply living with the illusion that material possessions, prestige, fame, a better house, or a newer car will make us content and fulfilled. They won't. They never have, and they never will. Money cannot buy us happiness; it can only buy us the quiet desperation of our choice.

The Culture and the Church

Rich was fortunate enough to learn the true value of money and possessions early on, and therefore, he was never encumbered with the need to acquire and achieve. Yet, as he left his home and Quaker roots, he encountered a Christianity that celebrated those very things. He was amazed to hear that many Christians had twisted the gospel into a message about financial prosperity.

Because Rich saw money as a distraction from the kingdom, he believed that if God made you rich He was not doing you a favor. Possessing wealth presented a great challenge to the believer, Rich thought; quite often discipleship meant enduring suffering, giving away one's treasures, and sacrificing for the good of others. It certainly meant letting go of the things that possess us, and for most of us, that would be the false sense of security that comes from relying upon money and possessions.

Rich understood Jesus' words so clearly, and he knew the truth of them in his own experience. The era that he grew up in—America in the 60s, 70s, and 80s—however, preached a message of materialism. Because contemporary culture lacks the inward disposition, it is no surprise that it lacks the outer lifestyle. The secular world does not understand the kingdom of God, and therefore, its only substitute is to serve Mammon, or the pursuit of wealth. In our culture we spend money we do not have to buy things we do not need in order to impress people we do not even like.[3]

> *The love of worldly possessions entangles the soul and prevents it from flying to God.*
> — Saint Augustine

As Rich said in the quote that opened this chapter, our culture worships "pleasure, leisure, and affluence." That is not surprising. But what was shocking to Rich was that many in the American church are doing the same things and, in Rich's words, "using Jesus as a vehicle for achieving all of that."

Rich thought just the opposite. Rich freely gave away his own possessions because he did not think of them as his. Likewise, he did not think of other people's possessions as theirs. He thought of everything as *ours*.

One time he was in Florida to do a concert, and he realized that he had not showered for several days. He called some people he had met only once and asked if he could come shower at their house. They welcomed him. After he finished showering, he got dressed, walked to the front door, thanked the people, and left. They were stunned. He left without staying and visiting. He just used their shower. Sam Howard says of the incident, "In his mind, there was nothing wrong with that. He needed a place to shower, and they had one. He used other people's possessions without feeling any obligation because that is how he would have treated them if they had needed to use his shower. With Rich there was no *mine* and *yours*; it was all *ours*."

While Rich lived with our family, I witnessed this many times. For example, each morning on his way to school he took a cup of coffee with him. After a month or so, I noticed that there were no mugs in our cupboard. The dishwasher was equally empty. When Rich got home that night, I said, "Hey, Rich, we seem to be missing all of our coffee mugs." He said, "Oh, I think I have some in my truck." We found at least twenty mugs sitting on the seat and floorboard. Some were broken, and some were not even ours. For Rich, material possessions were things to be used, not possessed.

To Identify with Jesus

As Rich discovered, the Bible is not ambiguous about issues of money and wealth. In fact, it challenges nearly every economic value of contemporary society. Jesus spoke to the question of economics more than any other single social issue.[4] Rich was aware of the implications of Jesus' teaching about the dangers—and futility—of seeking security in wealth. He said, "I think many people confuse being comfortable in their churches and society and feeling good about themselves, as being Christianity. Instead, I see Christianity as calling us *out* of our society—out of our conventions—for the sake of changing them for Him."[5]

What Rich wanted more than anything was to be faithful to Jesus, and for him, that meant caring for the poor. He said, "If I want to identify fully with Jesus Christ, who I claim to be my Savior and Lord, the best way I can do that is to identify with the poor. This, I know, will go against the teachings of all the popular evangelical preachers, but they're just wrong. They're not bad; they're just wrong."[6]

To follow Jesus meant to trust in Him, to believe that His words would always be true. Jesus said to seek first the kingdom, not the fulfilling of our needs. Rich wrote a song called "Hard" that contained a playful line about that kind of trust:

Well His eye is on the sparrow
And the lilies of the field I've heard
And He will watch over you and He will watch over me
So we can dress like flowers and eat like birds

He said, "I deliberately wrote that because I think what the gospel of Christ does, is it challenges us at every level."[7]

It challenges us to trust in God, not in our bank account, and that is precisely what Rich did. In the ancient liturgy of the Church, dating back centuries, we hear these powerful words: "Rich men have turned poor and gone hungry, but they that seek the Lord shall not be deprived of any good thing."

The things of this world are not ours to keep. We are merely stewards of them while we are here. Our pride sometimes leads us to say "mine" and "ours," when in reality everything is God's.

Rich kept an eye on eternity, and he knew that this world was not his home. When he received the news that his mentor, Maurice Howard, had died, Rich was scheduled to play a concert that evening. There he sang, for the first time in public, the great hymn by J. R. Baxter, "This World Is Not My Home." He sang it for Maurice, but it was also the cry of his heart. He sang it with tears running down his cheeks.

> *This world is not my home, I'm just a passin' thru,*
> *My treasures are laid up somewhere beyond the blue;*
> *The angels beckon me from heaven's open door,*
> *And I can't feel at home in this world anymore.*

If the world had ever been Rich's home before, it certainly was not now. Rich would live the rest of his life with a strong sense that treasures of this life are fleeting. He would spend his life storing up the treasures of heaven, which neither rust nor moth nor thief can steal or destroy (Matt. 6:19).

Money and Rich's Vocation

Rich's eternal perspective also gave him a different view of his vocation. He found working in the contemporary Christian music industry a difficult experience. Because it is a business as well as a ministry, it is concerned with making money. Because it is concerned with making money, it is always in a precarious position of compromise. The great danger in the Christian music industry is using people's need to hear the gospel and be inspired in order to make money. Rich wanted his own motivation to be pure.

Reed Arvin, who produced most of Rich's albums, says insightfully of him, "He separated himself from the careerists who thought it would be neat to make a little money out of Jesus."[8] Rich knew that making records costs money. He was also comfortable with the idea that someone made money from his records. That was the price for getting the message out to the world, which was really all he cared about. But he was uncomfortable with a subtly expressed emphasis upon financial success over the message of the music.

For many years Rich played and toured without ever having an album to sell. His uncle, Dick Lewis, says, "The one thing you could never motivate him with was money. In the early days, before his career took off, I told him he ought to do an album. Part of my reasoning was that he could finally make

> *One of the great dangers of having a lot of money is that you may be quite satisfied with the kinds of happiness money can give and so fail to realize your need for God. If everything seems to come simply by signing checks, you may forget that you are at every moment totally dependent on God.*
>
> — C. S. Lewis

some money, but I didn't tell him that. If I [had] said, 'You could make a lot of money from it,' he would have rejected it. So I said, 'You could reach a lot more people with your message if you had an album.' That is the only way I could get him to agree to it."

Eventually Rich did record an album, and eventually some Nashville music industry leaders heard it. Amy Grant recorded one of Rich's early songs, "Sing Your Praise to the Lord," and it went all the way to the top of the chart. But Rich was completely oblivious to the financial part of the music industry. His longtime manager, Gay Quisenberry, recalls that when Amy's management team called to get permission to record the song, "Rich said, 'OK, go ahead.' He got off of the phone and never even asked about the money. He thought he was giving it away."

Success Is Overrated

Rich knew that fame, like money, was fleeting. While he was passionate about his music, he had an incredible lack of interest in stardom. He once said, "I think success is overrated. It's something everybody goes after until they get it, then nobody knows what to do with it."[9] Rich didn't judge others who wanted fame. This was simply his conviction. Rich was well aware that he

I am amused to see from my window here how busily a man has divided and staked off his domain. God must smile at his puny fences running hither and thither everywhere over the land.

— Henry David Thoreau

was different in this regard: "It all seems ironic and weird to me. I'm thankful for it, but I never had any ambitions in Christian music."[10]

Rich had this attitude from the beginning. Dick Lewis remembers, "When he got the call from Nashville to come down and sign a big contract, he told them they would have to wait because he was going to camp up in Michigan to work with some youth, and he would get there when he got there. He made Nashville wait when most people would have jumped at the chance." He was more concerned with ministering to a group of young people than he was in furthering his music career.

After his first album, Rich was given one of the biggest opportunities in his career. He was invited to be the opening act on Amy Grant's *Unguarded* tour, which at the time was the largest Christian music tour in history. It was during that tour that he ended up meeting Gay Quisenberry, who would later become his agent and manager. Gay had never met Rich, and she tells the humorous—and very telling—story of how they met.

"In 1986 I was doing the booking for Amy Grant's *Unguarded* Tour. Rich Mullins was the opening act, but I had never met him. We were in Indiana for the first show I was working on, and we had this room for the artists to come and relax and have some refreshments. This guy comes in the door dressed in shabby clothes, and he looked like he hadn't bathed or shaved for days. I assumed he was a roady, or one of the truck drivers, so I went up to him and asked him to leave, telling him the food and drinks were for the artists. He said he was sorry and politely left and stood out in the hallway. An hour later the show began, and the announcer said, 'Please welcome Rich Mullins,' and out walks this same guy! After the show I apologized, and I asked him why he didn't tell me who he was after I told him it was for the artists, and he said he just assumed it was for the artists in Amy's band. For years to come, after we began working together full-time, he loved to remind me of our first meeting and how I ran him out of the room."

On that tour, Rich and Amy played a concert at Radio City Music Hall. For any performer, this was a great honor, and while Rich was excited, he wasn't overwhelmed. His sister, Debbie, says, "I went with a friend to see him when he was playing at the Radio City Music Hall. After the concert we were standing outside, and this white limousine someone had provided for [Rich] pulled up to take him back to the hotel. He told the driver to go on because he wanted to ride with the guys in the equipment van. We said good-bye and he left in the van.

"My friend said, 'Do you ever get tired of all these people treating your brother like he is some famous star, like he is any different [from] you or anyone else?' I said no. She asked why. I said, 'Because he is different [from] me or anyone else. I would have gotten in the limo.'"

While he was not overly impressed with having played at Radio City, he was proud of the opportunity. One day during the time that he lived with us I was talking with him up in his room, and I noticed that there was something that looked like a framed poster, turned backwards, leaning up against the wall. It had been sitting in the same spot for over a year. I asked if I could see it, and he reluctantly said I could. It was a framed photo of the marquee outside of the music hall that had the words, "Amy Grant and Rich Mullins in Concert Tonight." In his own way he was very proud of that day. Though he gave nearly all of his possessions away by the end of his life, I smiled when I was told that the photo was one thing he kept.

At times Rich faced challenges to his convictions from within the music industry. Gay Quisenberry remembers, "At one point, some people in the industry tried to make Rich a big star. They told him to lose weight, learn how to dance on stage, and write songs that were more upbeat. It really hurt his feelings. He told them no, and he stayed true to his art. Fortunately, Rich never got caught up in the star-making machine."

Gary Chapman adds, "That machine was something Rich was never going to be a part of. He flatly refused to be the by-product of someone else's vision. Two times he walked into the offices of major recording executives and told them off. And what was so funny was that in the long run, it made them love him more."

Nothing Is Really at Stake

It was also while on the *Unguarded* tour that Rich learned just how fickle applause is. Kathy Sprinkle attended one of the concerts on that tour and remembers how once Rich learned a powerful lesson about success: "That night he had a particularly good concert and was feeling very good about himself and how great it felt to hear all those kids screaming for him. We went for a walk near the end of Amy's set and returned through the parking lot as some of the teens from the concert were coming out. He accidentally bumped into a group of them. He had changed his clothes after his set, and he had on a ragged T-shirt and old jeans. As these kids walked by some of them laughed at him, and one said, 'Creepy old bum!'" That experience taught him a great lesson: the crowd can be cheering one minute and jeering the next.

Rich knew that there were more important things in life than his own success. Whether he was a star or an unknown, he was who he was. This attitude gave him an astounding freedom. He once told a group of journalists that they ought to write without the constraint of success:

> Even if [what you do] is a flop, tomorrow morning the sun's gonna come up just the same. Even if it's a flop, tomorrow evening it's gonna get darker and darker, and chances are there will be stars. The world will go right on no matter whether I succeed or fail. So I am suddenly free in a world of amazing possibilities. I can try anything I want to try because nothing is really at stake. And all this stuff we get caught up in, the idea of prestige, money, people recognizing you on the street. All those things become pretty secondary.[11]

It was the big picture, the grand scheme of it all, that freed him to try new things and not to be concerned with success because "nothing is at stake."

This freedom to fail allowed Rich to speak the words that were on his heart. He wasn't afraid to express opinions on any number of topics. Amy

> *The whole idea of St. Francis was that the Little Brothers should be like little fishes who could go freely in and out of the net. They could do so precisely because they were small fishes and in that sense slippery fishes. There was nothing that the world could hold them by; for the world catches us mostly by the fringes of our garments.*
>
> — G . K . C h e s t e r t o n

Grant remembers a time she invited Rich to play at a youth gathering in her barn. "I don't remember which political jag he was on that night, but he talked to the kids about things that had nothing to do with what we had gathered them for. Some of the people who helped us put it on were furious. I remember thinking he was like the wind that blows where it wills. The thing about Rich was that he was free to say what he wanted to say. He reminded me of a line from a Bob Bennett song that says, 'In the middle of this madness I am dancing.' He could go from being like a kid to being like a prophet from the Old Testament."

Ironically, the less Rich cared about success, the more successful he became. Michelle Fink, who worked for Reunion Records, recalls, "I once tried to track him down to tell him his song had hit number one on the charts. But he was singing on a street corner to a group of kids in Spain."[12] In the words of fellow songwriter, Wayne Kirkpatrick, "Rich was driven by the art and not the success of the art."

This "no fear" approach did not go unnoticed by people in contemporary Christian music. Phil Keaggy notes, "Rich could tell the truth in his music.

He didn't have any material gain that he was after; therefore he had nothing to risk and was able to speak honestly and clearly what he heard from God."

Rich's lack of fear enabled him to do things other people would never be able to do: at age thirty-four, leave the Christian music center of Nashville and go back to college.

Playing French Horn in the Pep Band

While most people try to get to Nashville in order to enhance their careers, Rich left Nashville, in some sense, to care for his own soul. Rich moved to Wichita first to be mentored by Maurice Howard, and second, to pursue one of his lifelong dreams: teaching music to Native American children. Rich needed to get a degree in music education, so he enrolled at Friends University.

> *A man should own nothing but his harp.*
> — Saint Francis

I was amazed at his ability to do this at this stage of his career. Here was an internationally known and revered Christian music star who was suddenly taking classes in music theory and singing in one of the college choirs. Rich wanted to be treated like any other student. I will never forget the first time I saw him onstage, singing with the choir, wearing an ill-fitting tuxedo. Even more startling was how much he was enjoying himself.

As a music education major, Rich was required to play a band instrument, so he chose the French horn because he had played it as a boy. Jennifer Jantz was a fellow music major who had many classes with Rich. She remembers, "Neither of us [were] very good at the French horn. . . . The other students in the band made fun of how bad we were. They said we sounded like sick cows. We were . . . required to play in the pep band at the football games. Rich didn't like it because of the music we played, but he did it anyway. We weren't good, but at least if you're trying to play a symphony, there is something beautiful in the music. . . . But here was Rich playing 'Proud Mary' with a French horn in a college pep band at a football game."

One evening during that time, Rich returned from Ireland where he had been shooting music videos. The next day I was sitting on the cold bleachers watching the football game when suddenly the pep band started play-ing. I looked over at them and there was Rich, blowing his horn. I remem-ber thinking, "One day he is treated like a big star, jetting across the Atlantic to make a video, and the next day he is playing the French horn in a pep band."

A Kid Brother in College

While he was at Friends University Rich started, along with Beaker, the Kid Brothers of St. Frank. They considered how to live the monk's tradi-tional vow of poverty. Rich said:

Having grown up Protestant, I was unfamiliar altogether with Saint Francis. Then I watched the movie, "Brother Sun, Sister Moon." The movie really clobbered me in a way that a really good movie can. I just became fascinated with the character of Saint Francis. What I saw in that movie was a man who had fallen in love with God, someone for whom God is everything. And that was one of those things that propelled me. I started reading about Francis and the Franciscan movement and asking the question, "What would it be like if we took the gospel that seriously?"

He saw in Saint Francis a person who was trying to live out the teachings of Jesus, and Rich found himself looking for ways to live out the Franciscan approach in the contemporary world. He goes on:

Beaker and I started looking at the three traditional monastic vows the Franciscans all take: The vow of poverty, the vow of obedience, and the vow of chastity. And we started saying, "What does that look like if you're not a monk?" We began to look at them in a broader sense rather than very specifically.

We came to believe that poverty is being a steward of whatever re-sources you have, as opposed to being the owner of those resources, that what is important is to recognize that everything belongs to God, and He allows us to be stewards of his gifts. And so rather than saying "OK, so we will just not own anything," we tried to look at everything that we own—our talents, our physical possessions—as being God's, and ourselves as being stewards of them.[13]

As a result, he and Beaker pooled their resources and asked a group of people to serve as overseers of their ministry. Rich hired Jim Dunning Jr. as his personal accountant. He asked Jim to take care of all of the money that came in and to give him and Beaker an allowance. All of the money that came in beyond that would be given away.

In time Rich would add a few others to the Kid Brothers. Mitch McVicker, whom Rich had met while at Friends University, moved with Rich down to the reservation in New Mexico, along with Eric Hauck and Michael Aukofer. These young men suspended the pursuit of their own careers to live and travel and perform with Rich. They formed their own version of a Franciscan community. Rich made sure that each of them received the same allowance he did, and he taught them how to live a life of simplicity in the ordinary events of life. In their daily devotions they often had someone read from the writings of Saint Francis.

Eric Hauck recalls, "Rich, by his own example, challenged me to live a life of simplicity and look beyond my own needs, to look not at what I can get but what I can give. Rich taught me that all I have is given to me by God to give to those that God has put in my path. I am not here to get from God, I am here to give from God."

Eric also tells a story about a time when Rich's actions spoke louder than his words: "One time we were in a fast-food restaurant, and there was this really poor family in line in front of us. Rich struck up a conversation with them, and they asked what he was doing in town. He told them he was a musician and was giving a concert. Rich invited them and told them he would make sure they got in for free. So they came, and Rich cleared out some seats right in the front row. I never knew what effect it had on that family, but it had an effect on me."

Traveling and playing music with Rich also had a big impact on Mitch McVicker. He remembers a key moment when all that Rich was teaching him became very clear: "One day we were driving through the really trendy part of Albuquerque, with all of these fancy movie theaters and book shops and cafes. As we were driving, he looked at me and said with a deep sadness, 'Mitch, the things of the world just don't satisfy.' I will always remember that."

Rich's freedom from the pursuit of material gain allowed him the opportunity to do what he wanted without the constraints of trying to build a career. His musical, *Canticle of the Plains*, was a radical endeavor. Instead of trying to convince a record company to produce it, he paid for the entire project himself, and he and his cowriters agreed that proceeds from the sale of the CD would go to the charity organization, Compassion International.

Free to Give

Saint Francis taught Rich that the things he owned were not his to possess but his to give away. Jim Dunning Jr. describes how Rich arranged his finances in order to do this: "He said he wanted to live on the average working man's wage, which at the time was about $24,000 a year. Obviously, his songs were being played on the radio, and his albums were selling well, so he actually made several times more than that. He told me he did not want to know how much he made because it would make it harder to give it away. What amazed me was that he actually lived on less than $24,000 a year. When he died . . . he had the equivalent of four months' salary that he had not spent."

> *Earn all you can,*
> *save all you can,*
> *give all you can.*
>
> —John Wesley

Rich frequently called Jim to ask about his financial situation, but not so he could buy things for himself. Jim says, "He called me one time and said, 'Do I have any money?' and I said, 'Sure, what do you need?' He then told me about a teacher he met [who] was trying to raise money to send some kids on a wilderness trip, and . . . he needed around three thousand dollars to do it. He said, 'Do I have enough to do that?' He had more than enough, but he didn't want to know how much. I told him, 'Yes,' and he said, 'Then can you send it to this guy?' And I did."

Is Poverty Spiritual?

While Rich admired Saint Francis, he chose, as he said, to look at the Franciscan vow of poverty in the larger context of stewardship. Rich did not believe that being poor was any more spiritual than being rich. He believed that the aim was not to be possessed by possessions but to be free enough to give them away. He flirted with the idea of poverty, but his uncle, Dick Lewis, taught him an important lesson. Rich told it this way:

Before I got into this music business, I was determined to live a life of dire and grinding poverty. I remember my uncle saying, "You are so proud of being poor—what's so great about poverty? You would do a lot better to be a little more industrious, a little more frugal. If you're really concerned about the poor, becoming poor isn't going to help them, it's just going to ease your conscience. If you're really concerned about the poor, go out and make a fortune and spend it on them."[14]

> Men rush toward complexity; but they yearn for simplicity.
>
> — G. K. Chesterton

To some extent that is what Rich ended up doing. He supported countless people and churches and ministries with the money he earned in the music business.

Rich did not believe that to be a truly committed Christian a person had to be poor. He came to the conclusion that God intends that we have adequate material provision. Simplicity is the right attitude: have and enjoy what we need, and praise God for it without being captive to it. That is how he chose to live.

Rich was not adverse to having nice things. In a journal entry quoted in an article called "In and Out of a Ragamuffin's Diary," he wrote, "Today I bought a far nicer cello than I can reasonably justify owning. I spent a lot of money today with school and the cello and all. I spent all day spending money only to come home to the best life possible which has nothing to do with money."[15] He did not believe that there was anything wrong with having material possessions, and at the same time he was aware of the potential danger in pursuing poverty as a way of life.

Rich's well-known choice of attire (tattered jeans, a T-shirt, and no shoes) was obviously not based on his economic situation. He could afford a better wardrobe. He wore what he did because he wanted to be on a comfortable level with his audience. Even then he noticed a potential danger. Kathy Sprinkle says, "The funny thing about the holey jeans was that he stopped wearing them all the time about two years before his death. Once in a while he would wear nicer clothes. When I asked him about it, he said, 'To take pride in poverty is equally as wicked as taking pride in wealth.'"

Eighty Square Feet

In the end Rich left this world with very little, which is exactly how he always said he wanted to leave it. Jim Dunning Jr. says, "In all the years I managed his finances, I noticed this: he never sold anything; he just gave things away. He gave away his vehicles, books, clothes . . . everything. Six weeks after he died, we went down to the reservation to get all of his possessions and give them to the family. When he moved down he used a twenty-foot truck. But by the time of his death, all of his possessions didn't fill half of the twenty-foot truck. We stored [them] temporarily in an eight-by-ten storage room. . . . I have clients who made less than Rich, who have seven-thousand-square-foot homes filled with possessions, and here was this guy who, in his entire life, could fill up only eighty square feet."

> *Be not anxious about what you have, but about what you are.*
> — Saint Gregory the Great

Rich had the same spirit as the apostle Paul, who said, "I have learned to be content with whatever I have. I know what it is to have little, and I know what it is to have plenty. In any and all circumstances I have learned the secret of being well-fed and of going hungry, of having plenty and of being in need. I can do all things through him who strengthens me" (Phil. 4:11–13). Rich knew the secret. He knew what it was like to have little and what it was like to have a lot. He learned how to enjoy all things through Christ, who gave him what he was really seeking—his "one thing," Christ Himself.

Instead of storing up treasures on earth, Rich is now enjoying the treasure he stored up in heaven. I've been told that the treasures we store up in heaven are the lives we helped to change, the moments we gave of ourselves for the good of others, and the things we gave away in order to help someone who was in need. If that is true, then Rich Mullins is today a very wealthy man.

8

Growing Young

Dealing with Sin and Temptation

I've gone so far from my home,
Seen the world and I have known
So many secrets
I wish now I did not know
'Cause they have crept
into my heart
They have left it cold and dark
And bleeding,
Bleeding and falling apart

Few people in the spotlight are as honest about the struggle with sin and temptation as Rich Mullins was. In very public arenas, such as concerts, he let people know that he, too, often struggled and failed. No matter how embarrassing the truth was, Rich simply could not pretend to be something he was not.

I was in Amsterdam, and there was so much sin all around us. After years of behaving myself as best as I could, I was really having to hang on for dear life. I was thinking, "No one would know. I could do anything I wanted to do. Wouldn't it be fun just to cut loose for a couple nights and misbehave as much as I want?" Fortunately, because I travel with my friend [and fellow band member] Beaker, and because he's not afraid to hold me accountable, I did not do anything. But I sure felt the temptation to toss out my morals for an evening.

A few days later, we were in Germany, sitting in a train station, assuming that everyone around us was German and did not speak English. We were having this totally candid conversation on a bench in the train station. I was talking very openly about some of those temptations. All of a sudden, this guy leans over and says, "Excuse me, but aren't you Rich Mullins?"

I went back over the conversation to see if I was going to admit to it or not. But I thought, this is good. A lot of times when we look at people we admire spiritually, we think they have arrived at this place where they cease to be tempted. The reality is, our faith may grow stronger over time, but the temptations never go away. It is hard for me to imagine that I will still feel tempted at 60, but when I was 20 I couldn't imagine I would feel such strong temptations as I do at almost 40.[1]

It was during this experience in Amsterdam, in the midst of the temptations, that Rich wrote the song "Hold Me Jesus."

One reason Rich was so open about his dealings with sin was that he knew he was not alone. Every human being battles temptation, yet seldom do we have permission to admit it. He was interested in shattering a popular but damaging illusion that "good Christians don't struggle with sin."

You know, a lot of people have this misconception that ministers and musicians and people who daily are talking about Christ and Christianity and that sort of thing really have no, or few, struggles. And I kind of had bought into that for a long time, thinking that, gee, by the time I'm in my mid-thirties, I should be pretty much too old to be tempted by anything. I have really had to come to terms with the fact that as long as I live, there will be temptations. And so . . . I just kind of got to a point where I was going, man, I don't know if I can make it. I don't know if I'm going to be able to live this close to falling all the time. But then I thought about the words of Paul, where the Lord spoke to Paul and said, "My grace is sufficient."[2]

Rich felt the pull of the flesh and the Spirit as we all do. His brother, Lloyd, recalls watching his brother struggle to be holy. One day, when he was seventeen, Rich took his two younger brothers, Lloyd and David, for a drive. Rich was young, but he was intent on living a Christ-centered life.

A few miles into the drive, the car broke down. Rich told his brothers— who were getting a little loud as they wrestled in the backseat—to be quiet so he could pray that the car would start. Rich prayed for a few minutes and then gently turned the key in faith. The car would not turn over. He began beating on the wheel and cursing. His brothers giggled in the backseat. He then calmed down and said, "We need to pray again, so be quiet." He prayed, tried the ignition, and again it did not start.

Rich began shouting and screaming at the car. This went on and on, with Rich alternately praying and cursing, until his dad, who had become worried about them, pulled up, walked over to the car, and with one turn of the key started the car. Lloyd says, "That story always sticks out in my mind when I think of Wayne. He could be holy and unholy at the same time."

As a young man, Rich was prone to believing that his faith was dependent on his sinning or not sinning. As he matured, Rich discovered that it was not his sin but God's all-sufficient grace that formed the foundation of his faith.

Rich also learned that the solution to sin was not trying harder but surrendering and running to Jesus. He said, "I always thought my parents didn't sin because they were just too old. When I was in Amsterdam, I was as old as my parents were when I used to think that. I guess you just think that as you live, you eventually outgrow temptation, and the reality is, you don't. You need Jesus just as much now as you ever did."[3] The temptations never cease, but more importantly, Jesus will never abandon us.

Sin Is Slop

Sin is very appealing on the front end. As Rich said in the opening story, he thought to himself, "Wouldn't it be fun just to cut loose for a couple nights and misbehave as much as I want?" No one would want to do something that isn't pleasurable. But the paradox is that sin is actually deadly. I have never had anyone—anyone—say to me, "After I committed the sin, I was really glad about it." Sin is not something that is really good that God, for some reason, has something against. Sin is toxic. We dwell in the ruins of a disordered world, one in which sin has many defenders but no defense. Sin is destructive by its very nature, but it must mask itself in the beginning in order to lure us until we are caught by the bait of present or promised pleasures. Rich understood the fact that sin is slop, that it destroys. In one of their songs, "Waiting," he and Beaker described the nature of temptation:

When a million voices whisper
And they tell me I should leave
Into the shadows that the moon casts
On these alleys and these streets
But I know that chasing shadows won't get me anywhere
'Cause I've been there

The voices whisper, calling us to leave God, to move into the darkness, but experience taught Rich that it is simply "chasing shadows" that "won't get me anywhere." He knew because he had been there.

In the song, "Growing Young," Rich and Beaker described how sin takes a toll.

Growing Young

I've gone so far from my home
Seen the world and I have known
So many secrets
I wish now I did not know
'Cause they have crept into my heart
They have left it cold and dark
And bleeding,
Bleeding and falling apart

And everybody used to tell me big boys don't cry
Well I've been around enough to know that was the lie
That held back the tears in the eyes of a thousand prodigal sons
Well we are children no more, we have sinned and grown old
And our Father still waits and He watches down the road
To see the crying boys come running back to His arms
And be growing young

I've seen silver turn to dross
Seen the very best there ever was
And I'll tell you, it ain't worth what it costs
And I remember my father's house
What I wouldn't give right now
Just to see him and hear him tell me that he loves me so much

And when I thought that I was all alone
It was Your voice I heard calling me back home
And I wonder now Lord
What it was made me wait so long
And what kept You waiting for me all that time
Was Your love stronger than my foolish pride
Will You take me back, take me back and let me be Your child
'Cause I've been broken now, I've been saved
I've learned to cry, and I've learned how to pray
And I'm learning, I'm learning even I can be changed

And everybody used to tell me big boys don't cry
Well I've been around enough to know that was the lie
That held back the tears in the eyes of a thousand prodigal sons
Well we are children no more, we have sinned and grown old
And our Father still waits and He watches down the road
To see the crying boys come running back to His arms
And be growing young

> *Only those who try to resist temptation know how strong it is. . . . That is why bad people know very little about badness. They have lived a sheltered life by always giving in. We never find out the strength of the evil impulse inside us until we try to fight it: and Christ, because He was the only man who never yielded to temptation, is also the only man who knows to the full what temptation means—the only complete realist.*
>
> *— C. S. Lewis*

Some people say, "What is so wrong with sin—you Christians are so repressed!" What they fail to see is that when we sin—any of us, Christian or not—we open a kind of "Pandora's Box," and we live with the consequences. Our lives begin to go badly. Though we may seek and experience God's forgiveness, we cannot erase the consequences of our actions. We learn secrets we will later wish we did not know; we will allow things to creep into our heart. There is no closing the box and hoping that it will go away. We live with it forever. A single moment of pleasure can lead to a lifetime of pain.

Lady Julian of Norwich said, "Sin has no substance. It is only known through the pain it causes." Rich understood this. He reflected in an interview:

My twenties were very, very disturbed years because it was the time of the real battle between my will to submit my will and my will to assert my will. I would flip-flop back and forth between saying, "Thank You, God, that you are the Lord and that I am not, because even though I am a rotten steward I would be a terrible Lord." And then I would say, "Yeah, but I am going to do this my way right now. I do love You, God, but I'm going to go my way, so look the other way a long time."

You know, by the time you've gone through that long enough, after you have beaten your head up against that wall for a good decade, you come out of it and you have accomplished all of the damage that God wanted to save you from. All you can do at that point is go, "Wow! I am so sorry that when You told me to walk in faith, I refused to do it. And now I know why You gave the commands that You gave. Now I know why You say what You say. And I wish that I didn't have to know that in order to obey it."[4]

We like to think that temptation will lessen as we age, that the struggle must be somehow easier for people who are in ministry or are serious about their faith. Even those who love God and long to be faithful can be lured by the fleeting pleasures of sin and by the constant desire to "run the show," to be their own god, and to do as they please. But experience teaches us the futility of this. We begin to see the wisdom of God, who gave us commandments not as a way of punishing us, or even testing us, but for our own good. God gives us His commandments because he wants to save us from being damaged.

We learn, certainly, by our mistakes, and many times we have to make them several times before we come to the point where, as Rich describes, we wish we didn't have to know it in order to obey it, where we would keep God's commands as naturally as we breathe. It is not a matter of being afraid of losing God's love, on the one hand, or feeling a license to sin because we are saved by grace, on the other hand. It is coming to realize that sin is simply not good, and our lives would be immeasurably better without it. As we mature in the faith, we come to the point where we can say, "Although I could sin, I am not planning on it. And if I don't sin, I won't miss it." That is spiritual maturity.

We call them the seven deadly sins for a reason: they are deadly to the human soul. Rich's friend and confessor, Father Matt McGinnis, says, "The world around us constantly feeds the seven deadly sins [pride, envy, anger, lust, sloth, greed, and gluttony], and tries to tell us that they are a real and natural part of life. In reality, they are animals that we feed. Rich tried hard, harder than many I know, to starve them."

Sin also ages us. In the story of Adam and Eve, there is a sense that prior to the Fall, they would live forever. As it was, they lived for hundreds of years. Each generation after theirs seemed to die a little sooner. Rich understood this in the same way as the believers did in the early Church, namely, that sin destroys us physically and works decay in our bodies. This is why he titled the song "Growing Young." When we sin, we grow old. When we repent, we grow young.

The Devil's Real Goal

What is it that God desires most from us? Many might answer, "He wants us to be holy. He wants us to sin less." Rich would disagree. He would say, "He wants us to be His." His trademark autograph was "Be God's"; not "Be good," but "Be God's." Being good in and of itself was not the main issue, though it was certainly a by-product of being in a close relationship with God. The main issue is surrendering our lives to God.

Understanding this helped Rich take his eyes off of sin and put them onto God. He described it this way:

I've been in and out of all kinds of things—like self-deprecation, self-interest, ego trips, alcohol, and other addictions. I've failed many times to avoid those kinds of temptations. But that's not what the devil was really interested in. What he was trying to do is make me feel apart from God. Now I know that what Satan would like most to take from us is our true knowledge of who we are—which is children of God.[5]

The goal of the enemy of our souls is to destroy our relationship with God by getting us to accept the lie that we are not loved. As strange as it may sound, the actual sin itself, while damaging to the person, is not the primary issue. Musician Billy Crockett, who played guitar on many of Rich's albums, noted, "We have a religious culture that tries to keep its nose clean all of the time, but in Rich you met someone whose allegiance was to something much greater than not sinning. His life was always pointing to a greater reality."

The devil tries to destroy our faith through our sin. He whispers, "See, you are a failure. God could never love you. You have sinned your way out of

> *A temptation arises: it is the wind.*
> *It disturbs you: it is the surging of the sea. This is*
> *the time to awaken Christ and let Him remind you*
> *of those words, "Who can this be? Even the winds*
> *and the sea obey him."*
>
> — S a i n t   A u g u s t i n e

His love. You promised you would never sin again, and you did. You let God down, and He is angry with you. It is best if you just run away." The desire of the devil is to see us become estranged and alienated from God.

The real concern is how we deal with sin: will it drive us deeper into more sin, seeking to assuage our pain and guilt, and farther and farther from God, or, will it compel us to turn to God and cry out for help, to ask for His mercy and draw closer and closer to Him, and live with increasing dependence upon His strength?

In the aftermath of sin, we feel "all alone," but the hound of heaven relentlessly bays upon our tracks, and we hear His voice calling us back home. We can only wonder why we waited to repent, but in our failure to return, we see that God never gave up, that He was waiting for us all of the time, proving to us that His love is stronger than even our pride.

Rich learned to recognize that the course of the battle depended on his willingness to ask for help. It is precisely here that we can win the battle with a word: "Jesus!" When we cry out to Jesus, the demons flee. Rich discovered that the name of Jesus can calm all of our inner storms. That's why, in the midst of the temptation in Amsterdam, he wrote this song:

Hold Me Jesus

Sometimes my life just don't make sense at all
When the mountains look so big
And my faith just seems so small

So hold me Jesus 'cause I'm shaking like a leaf
You have been King of my glory
won't you be my Prince of peace

And I wake up in the night and feel the dark
It's so hot inside my soul I swear
There must be blisters on my heart

Surrender don't come natural to me
I'd rather fight You for something I don't really want
Than to take what You give that I need
And I've beat my head against so many walls
I'm falling down, I'm falling on my knees

And the Salvation Army band is playing this hymn
and Your grace rings out so deep
It makes my resistance seem so thin

So hold me Jesus 'cause I'm shaking like a leaf
You have been King of my glory
won't you be my Prince of peace

The devil comes without invitation but leaves only when a power greater than himself commands him to do so. You and I do not have such power. But we do know, and in fact, we are *connected* to someone who does. When we call upon the name of Jesus, we are accessing the power of God. Calling on Jesus to help us overcome temptation may look weak to others, but it frightens the demons, who know it is their undoing.

If sin has any value, it is that it can drive us closer to God. Billy Sprague says, "We all have these double-sided personalities. We are pulled up by the Spirit and pulled down by the flesh, but the thing about Rich was that he never stopped fighting. His songs show us this restless pursuit. That tension gave him momentum and drove him toward faith."

Rich's brother, David, echoes the sentiment: "He would often say, 'Why can't God just take away my sinfulness? I know He is able.' But God didn't, and I think it was because his sinfulness drove him harder toward God." According to the lyrics of "Hold Me Jesus," Rich found that sin purged him and helped him know his weakness, which moved him to ask for mercy.

God allows us to sin and in fact, leaves us in our sin to break us of our vain affections and foolish pride. He does so in order to gather us back into Himself. God allows us to sin until we have grown weary and in pain, and like the prodigal, we want to "grow young" and come home.

A Near-fearless Life

One of the main obstacles to repentance is honesty. In order to come home, we have to come clean. Admitting failure is difficult because we are afraid that people think badly of us. Fortunately, this was not one of Rich's fears. He preferred to be honest rather than be fake, even if it meant having people think ill of him: "I think many times we are afraid to drop our guard because we're afraid that people will think that we are spiritually fake. Well, the truth is that we are. And so are they. And we're all trying to fake each other out."[6]

Rich had a strong sense of the reality of sin's presence in our lives. He knew that he was not alone, so he confessed his failures with little hesitation. His honesty often engendered a confession from the person to whom he was confessing. Rich realized that all of us have failed. Imagine if there were a device, a "sin detector," that we could attach to ourselves, which would begin listing off all of our sins in thought, word, and deed, and in what we have left undone. Most of us would cringe at the thought of being exposed, but Rich would have had no problem with it. As Mitch McVicker notes, "It was amazing how he was so open with his confessions. He told me that he figured if God knew his sins, then why should he worry about having someone else know them?"

This kind of honesty kept Rich from hiding from God, and in a sense, from others. He said:

I think one thing that is threatening to a good many of us is that we think, *If people really knew me they'd never believe in Jesus.* And I want to say, "No, that's exactly wrong." People will never know Jesus as long as we choose to hide ourselves. I don't think that necessarily means I need to go out and get on the radio to announce my private sins. I think that I can be very honest without being hurtful to people. [7]

Rich counted on the love of God and the mercy of Jesus at work in his life—two things that even his sin could not destroy. Instead of pretending to be perfect, he chose to admit that he sinned. And by bringing sin to the light, he created the possibility of healing.

Some have wondered, because of Rich's penchant for confession, if he was perhaps more of a sinner than most. In reality, his sins were no greater; he was just more open about them. The person he confided in most was his uncle, Dick Lewis, who points out, "We all have sins, we are all tempted, and we all have bad thoughts. . . . Wayne was just honest."

Rich's honesty paved the way for genuine self-knowledge. Gary Chapman grew close to Rich in a short time, and they shared their lives at a deep level. Gary notes, "Until you really become honest with your failures, you don't have any idea who you are. I don't know that I have met anyone who was more honest about his failures than Rich. He wasn't afraid to call it sin—he didn't try to cover it up or rationalize it. And in that revealing, he was able to live a near-fearless life. And that is something that I will continue to aspire to. . . . to live a life with no fear, to have that kind of perfect love that has done away with fear. I touch it now and then, and when I do, it is the sweetest experience I ever have."

Virtue Reality

Rich could live a "near-fearless life" because he chose not to put his faith in himself, in his own virtues, but in the grace of God. He knew that his failures could never keep him from God's favor, but equally as important, he knew that his successes could not secure it either. He once said:

I would rather live on the verge of falling and let my security be in the all-sufficiency of the grace of God than to live in some kind of

pietistic illusion of moral excellence—not that I don't want to be morally excellent, but my faith isn't in the idea that I'm more moral than anybody else. My faith is in the idea that God and His love are greater than whatever sins any of us commit.[8]

Though Rich strongly advocated the development of virtues and the destruction of vices, he knew too well that when we focus on them we can miss that which is higher and more important: the grace of God. If we concentrate on our vices, we can become easily discouraged; if on our virtues, we can easily become prideful. Either preoccupation will likely find us moving farther and farther from God.

Rich wrote an article about this problem in which he said:

Virtues are funny things. They are the fruit of faith and, whenever paraded, become parodies of themselves and the worst kind of vanity imaginable. When they are not the fruit of faith they become its greatest obstacle. Virtues are most vital when invisible and most sharply imaged when they are not the focus of our attentions. They are evidence of their Source (and ours) and not the generators of it (or us).[9]

Virtues are the fruit of faith, meaning they grow naturally from our relationship with God. They are not things that we can manufacture by our own effort; if they were, they would produce pride instead of humility. We receive virtues as gifts. Rich said succinctly, "I think that unless Christ is Lord of our virtues, our virtues become dangerous to us and dangerous to the people around us. I think that when Christ calls us to take up our cross, what He means is that you must die not only to whatever vices that are in your life, which He will eventually kill out, you must also die to whatever virtues that are in your life."[10]

Rich chose to put his faith in God's grace and nothing else, not his virtues or his talents. This made him a different kind of Christian artist. "Rich was a broken man," notes band member Phil Madeira. "So many public ministers hide their humanity. Rich failed to act the culturally expected role of a minister. His reliance on God's grace was one of desperation, which is really what everyone's should be. It's just that most of us rely on our successes and our works, houses on shaky foundations though they are."

To Be Holy Is to Be Human

Rich struggled with legalism, the idea that he must somehow earn God's love by doing the right things. Legalism is one of the great traps in the spiritual life and one that destroys more Christians than any other. Legalism is

> *Nothing so dispirits the demons as when their assaults are revealed. And nothing so heartens them as when their temptations are kept secret.*
>
> —The Desert Fathers

about rule keeping. It was the downfall of the Pharisees, but it is alive and well today. We see it in the attempt to define holiness on the basis of laws and rules.

This emphasis inevitably leads to hypocrisy. Rich believed that the legalistic approach to faith not only negates God's grace but deprives Christians of learning how to be human, which involves being honest and real. Actually, the journey toward being authentically human is more difficult than the path of legalism. Rich noted, "I think it would be really easy to say, 'I think what would really please God is if I don't dance, I don't chew, and I don't go with girls who do.' It would be easy to say, 'Oh, gee, I think what will really please God is if I become an evangelist and convert a thousand people.' It's much more difficult I think for me to become who I am and who He created me to be."[11]

Rich was never interested in what he termed "psychobabble," the vague pursuit of self-awareness. What he meant by becoming "who I am and who He created me to be" is found in the Book of Revelation.

One of the things I find beautiful in the book of Revelation is when Jesus says, "To him who overcomes I will give a white stone and on that stone is a name known only to the person who receives it and to Me." The white stone signifies victory and could very well hint at purity. The significant thing to me is there is a name on that stone that is the name Jesus knows me by. My mother does not know me by that name. My friends don't know me by that name. No one in this world, including myself, knows who I really am. I think that when we see ourselves in light

of Jesus, which will only happen when we give up ourselves and begin to seek Him wholeheartedly, then we will eventually grow into the person that He meant for us to be. When we see our name on that stone we'll say, "Wow, that's me! How did You know me when I couldn't even know myself?" For me, that's part of the goal of spiritual maturity.[12]

Growing into the person God created us to be, Rich thought, was the goal of the Christian life—not trying to sin less, but to be God's more. Mitch McVicker comments, "He would often say that the most holy thing he could do was to be completely human. He was more interested in being genuine and real than being crisp and clean on the outside. He said, 'God created us human, and that means struggling, falling, admitting it, and being healed.' A part of being holy means knowing that you are a struggling human and that you can be forgiven and healed by God. He always focused on the hope on the other side of the sin."

Rich became interested in the Christian discipline, often practiced in the Episcopal and Catholic churches, of receiving spiritual direction, the goal of which is holiness—but not in the traditional sense. He said in a magazine interview, "The spiritual director basically helps you sort through your own idea of who you are—to get past that and to come to experience yourself as God created you, and as God thinks you are, which would be the equivalent of holiness. To be who we are created to be would be to be holy."[13]

Coming to be who we are created to be is not an easy task, but one that requires a lot of interior work. In that same interview Rich went on to say, "Growing up Protestant, I always thought of a monastery as a place where cowards went, people who can't deal with the world. When you really begin to research some of this stuff, you find out that these are some of the bravest people. Anyone who decides to face themselves head-on is a very brave person."[14]

The Wisdom of Accountability

Rich decided to face himself head-on, to do the interior work of discovering who he was meant to be, when he was in his late twenties. He was working at a camp for youth, and he had grown weary of his own sinfulness. One Saturday morning he was sitting in the lodge with some of the other counselors, thinking about what he might do for the weekend. In truth, he was quietly considering ways he could get away by himself and sin as much as he wanted. He was really torn between the flesh and the Spirit.

Rich said at that moment an older man who worked at the youth camp as a supervisor walked into the lodge. The man kept to himself, got his coffee, and sat down to read his Bible. Rich had spent enough time with the man to know that he had lived a long and faithful life with Jesus. He said the man was very holy in an unpretentious way and that his presence in a room seemed to calm everything: "As I looked at him, I knew that I wanted to be like him one day." Then Rich had this thought: *If that is to ever going to happen, I am going to have to change.* He decided he had to leave the camp for the weekend and make some changes in his life.

Rich got in his car and started praying. He felt a desire to find someone to whom he could confess his sins.

I thought, I'm just going to stop and confess to the first preacher I see. The first church I go by, I'm going in there, and I'm going to tell everything. And I remember thinking, No, that's not what it means. Confession has to be something other than just saying words. It must be something more than just owning up to what you've done, even though that's a big part of it. I need to tell this to people whose opinion is most important to me.

Some of Rich's closest college friends lived in Cincinnati, so he immediately drove all the way from Michigan to Ohio. He didn't stop until he met with those friends and confessed his struggle. "It was one of the most liberating things I have ever done," he said. "It's not like I haven't been tempted since that time. It's not that I don't still deal with the same sorts of things. I still have to make right choices. I still have to flee temptation. But the power of that sin was broken."[15]

God has given us not only the power to call on His name, but also the grace of mutual accountability, the gift of being able to reach out to others and bring our sins to the light. One of the friends Rich confessed to was Gary Rowe. Remembering that event, Gary says, "Rich never hid anything. When he confessed to us that day, I remember feeling deeply honored by it." One of the paradoxes of confession is that we fear we will weaken our relationship with the person we confess to, but in reality, we strengthen the bond.

Father Matt McGinnis was someone with whom Rich felt comfortable sharing his struggles. Father Matt comments, "Often Rich would share very openly his sins and temptations. Some might think it would be embarrassing to hear the confessions of a person like Rich, or that it might make one think less of him. All I remember is feeling like I wanted to wash his feet because his humility made him so holy."

Rich not only made use of the gift of confession, but he also allowed himself to be accountable to people he trusted. He was accountable to close friends and writing partners Beaker and Mitch McVicker. Mitch remembers: "He prayed about his temptations a lot. He didn't allow himself to be alone too much because he thought it might be easier to sin and no one would know. Through it all, he taught me something important: that sin is not here one day, then gone the next. It is a daily process and a number of decisions. The struggle with sin lasts throughout our life, and each day and decision [are] a part of growing through it."

During the final two years of Rich's life, those of us who were close to him noticed that he was less tormented about his personal sins than ever before. Each time we got together, I noticed a real deepening of his relationship with Christ. It was clear Rich wanted to be a model of faith and purity to the young men he was leading, the Kid Brothers, and this desire spurred him on to holiness in the best sense of the word. He led them in daily devotions and took the lead in living up to the ideals of this little community.

Phil Madeira comments, "I think towards the end Rich seemed to have conquered some of his demons. He exercised wisdom in surrounding himself with people who were trying to live for Christ, and who, like Rich, knew how incapable they were of doing anything good apart from God's mercy."

Eric Hauck was one of the Kid Brothers who spent hours with Rich, driving to concert venues. "Rich saw the ultimate freedom that came from being totally up-front," Eric says. "Sometimes while we were just driving along, he would share openly, without hiding or putting on airs. He believed that being honest with a brother in Christ was a lifeline that helped him remain pure before God."

God has given us the wonderful gift of mutual accountability, but too few of us actually take advantage of it because we are afraid of what others will think of us if we share our doubts, fears, concerns, sins, and failures. The devil is counting on this fear preventing us from becoming transparent with one another. He knows that if we confess, we will be healed, and in time, become stronger than ever before.

"Temptation discovers what we are," said Thomas à Kempis. It exposes our base of strength. Are we running our lives out of our own resources, or are we looking to God to provide and to protect us?

The Bottom Line

Temptations should not frighten us, Rich learned. In a sense, to be alive is to be tempted. The only thing worse than temptation is not to be tempted at all, for then we can rest assured that we are no threat to the enemy. We are tempted because we are valuable.

And our temptations can teach us. They can help us learn the art of dependence upon God. In time we can learn to respond to temptation with Rich's simple prayer: "Hold me, Jesus."

9

Brother's Keeper

Learning to Love One Another

I will be my brother's keeper

Not the one who judges him

I won't despise him

for his weakness

I won't regard him

for his strength

I won't take away his freedom

I will help him learn to stand

And I will, I will be my

brother's keeper

Rich Mullins believed that his life and his music would be judged by one thing: love. He became convinced that the only thing that matters is love—not the emotional feeling but the acts of love that we do in the mundane moments of life. Jesus said, "By this everyone will know that you are my disciples, if you have love for one another" (John 13:35). Rich knew love was a hard standard.

Someday we'll be called to give an account and . . . I don't think our crown will be the words we wrote; I think it will be how we have built up the body of Christ, how we have torn down walls of suspicion and walls of fear, how we have shed light on false doctrines, how we've been encouraging truth and how that affects lives, and how we made Jesus visible.

I've never been tempted to write about stuff that I didn't think would help us, because I do believe someday I will die and there will be a judgment. . . . Jesus talked of judgment as a matter of what we do with our lives: Did we visit those in prison, did we give to the poor? You know I used to think it was for the advantage of the people in jail and for those people who were naked and hungry. Now I think that He asks us to do that not so that they can be saved, but so we can be. If we want to meet Jesus it won't likely be at church, although I'm a big believer in going to church. I think that when we meet Christ it will be somewhere outside the camp. It will be where people have been marginalized, people who have been literally imprisoned. We will meet Him where we least expect to.[1]

Called to Be Lovers, Not Saviors

The applause of the audience fades into the night. Only one thing endures: our acts of charity. Rich believed this, and he spent his life learning how to love other people.

> *I think we must look Christ in the face, whose mercy we have received, and tell him whether we will join heart and soul and body and circumstances in the march to publish his mercy to the world.*
>
> — William Booth

One of the first things he learned about loving others was that he must accept people without judging them. Apparently Rich was successful at this; comments fellow musician and friend Phil Keaggy, "He understood and accepted people. Saint Paul called himself 'the chief of sinners.' I think Rich believed that about himself, and therefore, he had no self-righteousness. To me he was a broken man with a touch of Peter, Paul, and Francis. You could see this in the fact that he seemed to enjoy the company of ordinary people."

Because of his awareness of his own sinfulness, Rich was not prone to judge others. He was indeed aware that he was not a man "without sin"; therefore, he had no stones to throw. But his understanding of love was deeper than merely not throwing stones. For Rich, it also meant learning to accept people as they are, to embrace them even with their flaws, to love them without trying to fix them. He wrote:

God has called us to be lovers and we frequently think that He meant us to be saviors. So we "love" as long as we see "results." We give of ourselves as long as our investments pay off, but if the ones we love do not respond, we tend to despair and blame ourselves and even resent those we pretend to love. Because we love someone, we want them to be free of addictions, of sin, of self—and that is as it should be. But it

**might be that our love for them and our desire for their well-being will
not make them well. And, if that is the case, their lack of response no
more negates the reality of love than their quickness to respond would
confirm it.[2]**

Quite often we extend love toward people because we want to change
them. Rich believed that we ought to love without any requirements. We are
called, he thought, to love for the sake of love, with no expectations. Even if
a person fails to respond to our love, our kindness, or our forgiveness a
thousand times, we are called to keep on loving. Rich discovered that to love
this way gives the freedom to love perfectly.

For Rich, loving others meant not judging or trying to force them into
being what he wanted them to be. His understanding of this led him to
write a song with Beaker to communicate this message of unconditional
love.

Brother's Keeper

Now the plumber's got a drip in his spigot
The mechanic's got a clank in his car
And the preacher's thinking thoughts that are wicked
And the lover's got a lonely heart
My friends ain't the way I wish they were
They are just the way they are

I will be my brother's keeper
Not the one who judges him
I won't despise him for his weakness
I won't regard him for his strength
I won't take away his freedom
I will help him learn to stand
And I will, I will be my brother's keeper

Now this roof has got a few missing shingles
But at least we got ourselves a roof
And they say that she's a fallen angel
I wonder if she recalls when she last flew

There's no point in pointing fingers
Unless you're pointing to the truth

Rich described how he wrote the song: "I used to live with James Bryan Smith and his wife, Meghan, and their little boy, Jacob. And Jim—I call him Jim—was working on a book called *Embracing the Love of God* at the time. And so, me and him and Beaker were sitting out on the front porch talking about the whole thing of trying to love people and not expect anything out of them. And Jim went in to make us some coffee, and when he came back out, me and Beaker had written this song."[3]

For several months during that time, our conversations were all about God's love, how we are called to accept our acceptance with God, and in response to that love, accept and forgive and care for others. Out of those discussions came a book from me and a song from him. It took me over a year to write the book; it took Rich five minutes to write the song, and that song says everything both of us were trying to say.

The song begins with an honest appraisal of the human race: behind the facade, we are all sinners, we are all imperfect. Plumbers shouldn't, but they sometimes have leaky faucets; mechanics shouldn't, but they often have cars that need repair; and preachers shouldn't, but they can have wicked thoughts just like anyone else, and often do. The song offers Rich's confession that the people in his life were as weak and ignorant and prone to sin as he himself was. It is actually freeing to admit this. Rich himself realized, "If I have to have perfect people in order to have friendships, I'm going to be a very lonely guy."[4]

So, what are we to do with the awareness that our friends and neighbors are not perfect? This is what Rich thought we ought to do: "I will be my brother's keeper. Not the one who judges him. I won't despise him for his weakness. I won't regard him for his strength. I won't take away his freedom. I will help him learn to stand." In short, we are to care for those who are near us and never judge them. This was exactly how Rich lived. He was never impressed by people's accomplishments or talents, and he was never discouraged by their failures or weaknesses.

Alyssa Loukota, who worked closely with Rich for several years, calls him "an extremely loyal friend." She says, "Rich felt that if Jesus could hang in there with him, then he ought to hang in there with everyone else." Other friends noticed Rich's humility as well. While at Cincinnati Bible College, Rich lived in a community house with the other members of his singing

> *You should not let a single person in the world, whatever sin that person may have committed, come before your eyes and depart without having found mercy with you. And should that person not ask for mercy from you, then you must ask it of him. And were that person to come to you a thousand times, continue to love them so as to lead them back to the right path. Always have compassion, for all of us have sinned.*
>
> — Saint Francis of Assisi

group, Zion. Mark Lutz remembers, "Rich would pick up strays, these cast-off people, and invite them to live with them. He would bring hitchhikers home all the time. When I was a freshman, my roommate and I were real outsiders. One day Rich came over to our room and we chatted. I was one of those underdog people. My folks were divorced and Bible college felt strange to me, and he picked up on that. He reached out to me and drew me into his circle of friends."

In many ways Rich's best quality was his nonjudgment. He knew that we often wear masks with each other, afraid to let others see who we really are. He could look beneath the mask and affirm the person we really are, the real us, not the one we show in public. Jesus said, "Do not judge, so that you may not be judged" (Matt. 7:1). When we meet a person for the first time, we fear that we will be judged, that the person will see through our charade and find our faults. But Rich saw through the pretense. In "Peace," a song about God's invitation to Communion, he and Beaker wrote of the mercy that supersedes judgment:

Though we're strangers, still I love you
I love you more than your mask
And you know you have to trust this to be true
And I know that's much to ask
But lay down your fears, come and join this feast
He has called us here, you and me

. . . And though I love you, still we're strangers
Prisoners in these lonely hearts
And though our blindness separates us
Still His light shines in the dark
And His outstretched arms are still strong enough to reach
Behind these prison bars to set us free

> *You never become truly spiritual by sitting down and*
> *wishing to become so. You must undertake something*
> *so great that you cannot accomplish it unaided.*
> — P h i l l i p s   B r o o k s

One of the most beautiful lines in "Brother's Keeper," and one that is easy to miss, is this: "And they say that she's a fallen angel; I wonder if she recalls when she last flew." He is describing a young, beautiful woman who has made some terrible choices, whose life has become a tragic waste; her beauty is fading along with her hopes; people whisper behind her back. This happens all too often. But Rich looks at this fallen angel and asks, "I wonder if she recalls when she last flew." Meaning, "Does she know the beauty of who she really is, independent of her mistakes?" When I hear that line, I think of how Mary Magdalene must have felt when she saw the tender eyes of

Jesus, who, when he looked at her, did not see a prostitute or an evil person, but an angel. No wonder she followed Jesus. No wonder the lost and broken crowded around Rich Mullins.

Rich took for granted that every person has defects that he would prefer to hide, but he chose not to dwell on them. Jennifer Jantz, a student at Friends University, recalls, "During spring break one year, five of us from college went out with Rich to the reservation to check it out and see if Rich and Mitch really wanted to live there. We were just a bunch of immature college kids, and I wondered why he put up with us and why he would allow us to spend so much time with him. In the end I think it was because Rich was great at finding the good in people and focusing on that instead of on their weaknesses. I realized later that he was once our age, and he knew that we would one day grow out of being so self-absorbed."

In our neighbors we should observe only what is good.

—Saint Jeanne de Chantal

Because of this quality, people felt comfortable with Rich. His editor at *Release* magazine, Roberta Croteau, traveled with Rich and noticed, "Some people are just born with people being drawn to them. When we were in Bogota, people just flocked to him and followed him everywhere, and he wasn't even that famous. The kids only knew he was a person who helped them build their school."

More Than Words

Not judging others is only one dimension of loving. Rich knew that love also entails being kind, showing hospitality, and giving others all that we have to give. Rich believed that if we have to tell people that we love them, we probably don't.

Rich also believed that the love of God becomes a reality for us when we see this kind of love from the people around us. He traced his own conversion to the love he saw in the lives of faithful women and men:

I am a Christian because I have seen the love of God lived out in the lives of people who know Him. The Word has become flesh and I have

encountered God in the people who have manifested (in many "unrea-sonable" ways) His presence—a presence that is more than convincing—it is a presence that is compelling. I am a Christian, not because some-one explained the nuts and bolts of Christianity to me, but because there were people who were willing to be nuts and bolts. Through their obedience to the truth and not necessarily through their explanation of it, they held it together so that I could experience it and be compelled to obey.[5]

In terms of evangelism, Rich discovered that the best way to communicate the gospel is through acts of kindness and love. He believed in the dictum of Saint Francis: "Preach the Gospel wherever you go, and use words only if necessary."

Rich preached the gospel without words many times. His cousin, Matt Johnson, comments, "His acts of love were small but profound. He would buy me a book, and it was always the perfect book. One small gesture that really had an impact on me was the time he gave me time off from the tour to be with my fiancée. As I left he said, 'You need to go because love is something you build.'

"As a roadie, I appreciated the fact that [Rich] always helped set up the stage. I never saw another big-name Christian musician do that. We all knew that each night he had to sound good, he had to be profound, and he had to be 'on,' and we also knew that he was often tired. But nevertheless, there he was, each night, helping us to set up the stage."

Gary Chapman also toured with Rich and witnessed the same spirit. "I noticed that he treated everyone the same, from the common workers to the stars. There is a pecking order on tours, and Rich made sure that this was abolished. I saw him live his life as a service. People preach that, and it sounds good when you say it, but it can't ever sound as good as it looks when you actually see it happen. He lived a life based on serv-ice. He hooked up a microphone because it was there and needed hook-ing up."

Rich never thought of his music career as a vehicle for self-promotion. He often hired inexperienced musicians not only to give them an opportu-nity but also to be able to minister to them. Singer Ashley Cleveland, who was the opening act for one of Rich's tours, recalls: "On the tour Rich asked how he could help me. I asked for a guitar technician because I change guitars so much in my concerts. He said, 'Done.' But then the first night this young

> *Do not waste time bothering whether you "love"*
> *your neighbor; act as if you did. As soon as we do*
> *this we find one of the great secrets. When you*
> *are behaving as if you loved someone, you will*
> *presently come to love him.*
>
> — C. S. Lewis

man came out and handed me a guitar, and as I played it, it was badly out of tune. The same with the second night, and the third, and for several nights. Finally, I said to this young man, 'Have you ever been a guitar technician before?' He smiled and said, 'No.' So I asked Rich, 'How come you hired this guy? He's never done this before.' And he said, 'I just really felt that this kid needed mentoring.' That was how he always was. His career took a backseat to the needs of others. Ever since then I have looked at my own life and my own career in a different way."

Rich loved to see other people grow. Reunion Records executive Don Donahue remembers, "I saw one of his last concerts and I was blown away with how good it was. I told Rich afterwards, and he said, 'Will you tell these guys how great they did?' He wanted those young guys to be affirmed for what they were doing [by] someone other than him. He was a great leader. He wanted them to know they did good because he was rooting so hard for them."

Rich followed Saint Paul's advice: "Let love be genuine; hate what is evil, hold fast to what is good; love one another with mutual affection; outdo one another in showing honor" (Rom. 12:9-10). One of the Kid Brothers, Eric Hauck, recalls how much time and energy Rich spent helping them: "I was really impressed that when we got together on the reservation for three weeks of rehearsal before the tour, we spent two weeks working on Mitch [McVicker]'s opening part of the concert and only one preparing for our part

> *In the Christian sense, love is not primarily an emotion but an act of the will. When Jesus tells us to love our neighbors, he is not telling us to love them in the sense of responding to them with a cozy emotional feeling. You can as well produce a cozy emotional feeling on demand as you can a yawn or a sneeze. On the contrary, he is telling us to love our neighbors in the sense of being willing to work for their well-being even if it means sacrificing our well-being to that end.*
>
> — Frederick Buechner

with Rich. You would think a big star like Rich would be only interested in his own career, but instead he invested in us. If it weren't for Rich, we wouldn't ever have had a chance."

It Isn't Love Until You Act

Loving others wasn't something Rich found too costly or uncomfortable to live out. He genuinely enjoyed seeing others happy. In his song, "A Place to Stand," Rich said,

> *There's a lot of love locked up inside of me*
> *That I'm learning to give*

He expressed that love in a number of concrete ways to a variety of people because he believed that love is real only when it is given freely and without expectation of return. He said, "Love is a virtue and not a feeling. It is fed and fired by God—not by the favorable response of the beloved. Even when it doesn't seem to make a dime's worth of difference to the ones on whom it is lavished, it is still the most prized of all virtues because it is at the heart of the very character of God."[6]

"Rich believed that love wasn't love until you acted," Mitch McVicker says. "He talked a lot about love, but he loved even more. Not in flowery ways. One of the ways he showed love to me was by giving his time and his energy to me. It was the gift of himself that was loving." His love, as Mitch notes, was seldom "flowery" but was often seen in the small things in life. Rich's college friend, Sam Howard, recalls a time he visited Rich: "I went down to Tennessee to visit him, and he tried to make a cake for us. It was awful, but it was nice to see him try."

One day a close friend of mine, Richard J. Foster, stopped by the house for a visit when Rich was still living with us. Though the two had never met, they instantly struck up conversation because Rich was wearing a T-shirt with a picture of the great Native American leader, Chief Joseph, on it. Foster said, "Chief Joseph was my childhood hero. That is a great shirt." Rich responded, "Here, you can have it." I watched in amazement as he literally gave him the shirt off of his back. I knew that the T-shirt meant a lot to Rich, but it meant even more to him to see someone else enjoy it.

While he was a student at Friends University, I watched him minister to other students. Jennifer Jantz sat next to Rich in their 8:00 A.M. band class. She remembers a small act of kindness that had a big impact on her: "One day, out of the blue, he brought me a cappuccino from a convenience store. After that first time, he brought me one every day. . . . If he thought you might like something, he wanted you to have it."

Rich touched my life with kindness too. For example, when my wife and I got engaged, we noticed that the clock read 11:11 P.M. We have always joked about how I popped the question at that exact minute. Rich heard us tell the story and apparently never forgot it. Several members of his band told me that if they were riding with Rich in his jeep and his dashboard clock flashed

11:11, Rich said, "Hey, let's stop and pray for Jim and Meghan." He never told me about this practice, but then again, he did not do it to impress anyone. He did it out of his love for us.

Real Spirituality

Rich believed that the most spiritual activities are the routine ones. He said,

A spiritual thing is folding your clothes at the end of the day. A spiritual thing is making your bed. A spiritual thing is taking cookies to your neighbor that is shut in or raking their front lawn because they are too old to do it. That's spirituality. Getting a warm, oozy feeling about God is an emotional thing—there is nothing wrong with it—I think there is nothing more practical than real spirituality.[7]

We tend to think that our most spiritual moments are the ones we spend in churches or in private prayer. Rich felt that the ordinary events of daily life were the stuff of Christian formation.

It was for this reason that he felt that every Christian was in ministry. Many believers make a strong separation between the spiritual and the secular, but Rich was often frustrated by this kind of dichotomy. He said to a group of Christian writers:

I would like to encourage you to stop thinking of what you're doing as ministry. Start realizing that your ministry is how much of a tip you leave when you eat in a restaurant; when you leave a hotel room whether you leave it all messed up or not; whether you flush your own toilet or not. Your ministry is the way that you love people. And you love people when you write something that is encouraging to them, something challenging. You love people when you call your wife and say, "I'm going to be late for dinner," instead of letting her burn the meal. You love people when maybe you cook a meal for your wife sometime because you know she's really tired. Loving people— being respectful toward them—is much more important than writing or doing music.

. . . If you are a Christian, ministry is just an accident of being alive. It just happens. And I don't know that you can divide your life up and

say, "This is my ministry" and "This is my other thing," because the fruits of Christianity affect everybody around us.[8]

Rich's friend, Tom Boothe, remembers Rich living out his words when Tom visited him on the reservation. "At the time Rich and Mitch

> *It is necessary to try to obey the commandments of God. And just exactly what are we to do? Nothing in particular—only those things which present themselves to us in the circumstances of daily life, those things required by the every day happenings we all encounter.*
>
> — S a i n t   T h e o p h a n

lived in a trailer. Rich demanded that I take the bedroom. He said he would sleep on the floor. It was a real lesson to me on hospitality. He taught me that you don't just give people something; you give them the best you have."

The Ministry of Music

Music was the primary way Rich ministered to people, even though he sometimes doubted its effectiveness: "I think I have a limited ministry potential in the Christian music business," he said, "because the people who changed my life were not the people who sang to me. They were the people who loved me."[9] Yet countless people across the world have been blessed by Rich's music. He provided words for inexpressible feelings, bared his own soul, and inspired active faith. Amy Grant comments, "I am so moved by his songs, I think, because there are levels of honesty in any song, and Rich was able to be as honest in his music as he was with himself—which was to the highest degree. His music truly connected him to people he had never met. I always feel braver when I listen to his songs."

The power of Rich's music to communicate love was never more real for me than in one particular song he wrote about our daughter. One week before she was due, we received the terrible news from our doctor that the little girl inside Meghan appeared to have a number of birth defects that would prevent her from living; in fact, it was unlikely she would even survive her birth. Our world collapsed. We started planning her funeral. As doctors performed a C-section, we prepared to say hello and good-bye in the same breath.

> *The way to love anything is to realize that it might be lost.*
>
> — G. K. Chesterton

Somehow Madeline did survive. Within a few days we were allowed to take her home, but we were told that she would probably die within a short time. As soon as he heard our news, Rich called. I will never forget our conversation. Within a few minutes I was crying and pouring out my heart. Rich said absolutely nothing. Though this is often an appropriate response, I wondered after we finished talking, *Does this guy really care?* I would learn that he cared a great deal—too much, perhaps, to say in words.

Madeline continued to defy the doctors' prognosis. Rich, who was living on the reservation then, came to stay with us several times, and I noticed that he was getting attached to her. On one of his visits, he called and said, "Hey, I wrote a song for Madeline. Can I stop by to play it for you?" To our surprise he brought his whole band to our house and played it for us in the living room. It was a beautiful lullaby about how heaven sees those who are frail and how God is deeply moved by the prayers of the weakest of the weak. Rich went on to play the song in his concerts during his final tour. He introduced it this way:

> This is a song I wrote for a little girl who wasn't supposed to get born because the doctor said she would never survive the birth. She was born, and a couple days later he said, "Well, she won't survive the week." She survived the week, and a month later he said, "She won't live a year." Now after about sixteen months, she weighs about twelve pounds. When

she sleeps, she folds her hands like she is praying. We all think that she's praying for us. So this is a song I wrote for her. [10]

Madeline fusses
Madeline laughs
The angel who watches says
"Hey, look at that!
There's your faith—
Mountains will shake
'Cause God gladly bends
Just to hear Madeline
When she prays."

Madeline stretches
Madeline kicks
Angels in heaven say
"Hey, look at this!
There's your faith—
Mountains will shake
'Cause God gladly bends
Just to hear Madeline
When she prays."

And the only angels that I've ever seen
Look like tears on the face of the sky
Though it sure breaks your heart to see heaven all streaked up
With sorrows like theirs—so you know all the while

From where cobbles are golden like emeralds shine green
From where gems stud the streets and the walls
God looks out a window at us just to see
If anything frail as a sparrow should fall

God gladly bends
Just to hear Madeline
When she prays

Rich would whisper his prayers into Madeline's ears and though she was profoundly deaf, he believed she had, as he put it, "real pull with God." Only Rich Mullins would have a prayer partner who couldn't speak or hear.

Madeline not only prayed for Rich, but Rich prayed for Madeline. Eric Hauck remembers, "We had devotions every day as a band, and every day we prayed for Madeline. We always got updates about how she was doing—if she was in the hospital or at home—and what her condition was. Devotions were never over until we prayed for Madeline."

Six months after Rich's death, Madeline died. Some of the Kid Brothers attended the funeral and played her song. In the midst of the most painful time in my life, I was strangely comforted by the thought that Rich and Madeline were now exploring heaven together.

Compassion for the World

In Rich's travels he visited other countries and areas in America where poverty had created desperate situations. South America and a Native American reservation in the southwest United States particularly worked their ways into his soul. He longed to do something to better the living conditions in those places. As a result, he began working with an organization called Compassion International. Compassion offers sponsorship for children in developing countries. Through a small monthly donation, sponsors provide for children's basic needs, including food, clothing, and education. Sponsors receive pictures of the children they support and are encouraged to write them letters.

Rich described the way he started working with Compassion:

I went on a trip with Compassion. I appreciated a lot about the organization. But I got to Guatemala and actually met kids who had letters from their sponsors put in little boxes that were almost like shrines. These kids had memorized the letters, and they would give you the letter and then they would quote it word for word, what was said.

And I talked to a mother of about three kids who are Compassion-sponsored . . . and found out about how one of her children was stolen from her, and how excited she is that her children are getting an education—and that they might be able to do something besides live in front of

a cement wall and make tortillas from about three in the morning until about nine in the evening.

And when I saw the impact that Compassion had on her, not just on the kids who are being sponsored, but on the people around them, when I talked to people who are not even yet Compassion-sponsored children

> *To love at all is to be vulnerable. Love anything, and your heart will certainly be wrung and possibly broken. If you want to make sure of keeping it intact, you must give your heart to no one, not even to an animal. . . . lock it up safe in the coffin of your selfishness. But in that casket . . . it will change. It will not be broken; it will become unbreakable, impenetrable. . . . The only place outside Heaven where you can be perfectly safe from all the dangers and perturbations of love is Hell.*
>
> — C. S. Lewis

but who were aware that there were people that had resources that were responding to the needs of those people there, all of a sudden I went, "Wow!" Suddenly I switched from thinking, *Yeah, this is a great idea* to this being a passion of mine.[11]

Rich was so moved that he gave an entire tour to raise money for a little church in Bogota, Colombia.

On a trip to Bogota, Colombia, with Compassion International, Rich soon became friends with a pastor named Carlos, who was trying to build a church. Pastor Carlos recalls, "I was very depressed (to know about Rich's death) because to us he was a person who was very thoughtful and well-received and God put it in his heart to help us." [12]

Alyssa Loukota, who worked with Rich and met him through his work with Compassion International, described Carlos's church: "They sort of had a cement block [building] and they were trying to have a school there and a

> *The bread that you store up belongs to the hungry;*
>
> *the coat that lies in your chest belongs to the naked;*
>
> *the gold that you have hidden in the ground*
>
> *belongs to the poor.*
>
> — S a i n t   B a s i l

church. And there was nothing else in this area—no school, no churches. When Rich came back, he said, 'I want to spend my next tour raising money for that pastor to have what he needs.'" That is exactly what Rich did. Pastor Carlos, reflecting on the work Rich did for them, and the fact that he is now in heaven, said, "He scattered seed and then he left, but now the planter is receiving marvelous fruit." [13]

During many of his concerts on that particular tour, Rich also presented audiences with an opportunity to sponsor children. Though a number of Christian musicians are involved with Compassion, Rich became one of ministry's most effective advocates.

Rich himself sponsored three children, and he had the privilege of actually meeting one of them, a little girl named Alexandra, when he was in Bogota. Today Alexandra says, "I loved him a lot. When he came here, he gave me this medallion, which I still remember him by and guard it. I have photos with him. He talked to me about his ministry. Through him I came to know God. He worked with the poor people in need. To him the Word of God was important. I love him very much. And even though he has passed away, he will always be in my memories."

There are many children in Bogota who remember Rich. Another of those children, a little boy, said, "Rich taught us first of all to love and to be loved.

> *One secret act of self-denial, one sacrifice of inclination to duty, is worth all the mere good thoughts, warm feelings, and passionate prayers in which idle people indulge themselves.*
>
> — C a r d i n a l   J o h n   H e n r y   N e w m a n

He taught us to respect others and to love each other as brothers. I am certain that where God has him, it is going to be a good place for him to be, because he was a man that did wonderful things in this world." [14]

After a few visits to the Native American reservations, Rich felt the same concern he felt for those who lived in oppressive conditions in other parts of the world. What was staggering to Rich was that the Native Americans were . . . Americans. They were citizens of the wealthiest country in the world, and even more, they were the original inhabitants of this nation. As he spent more and more time with them, Rich felt his heart breaking. Alyssa Loukota said, "It was because of Rich that Compassion began its work in the USA, the Native work in particular, which Rich did exclusively at the end."

During the last two years of his life, Rich lived on a reservation. He went there to teach music to children, but many people wondered if he was on a quest to convert the Native Americans. Mitch McVicker recalls, "Rich once said to me, 'People talk about me going out to the reservation to save the Navajos, but the opposite is what is happening. They are blessing me. I'm being changed by them. I'm the one being saved by coming here.'"

Rich invested himself deeply into the culture and gave of his time and energy to do what he could to help the people on the reservation, especially the children. Eric Hauck remembers, "Rich had a tremendous love for the kids. Whenever we were rehearsing down on the reservation, if any of the native kids came in to see Rich—and they often did—he would always stop and spend time with them, no matter how pressed we were for time. He would have us travel all the way out into the country to play for a small group of kids in a school on one of the reservations. He always did it for free.

> *The best moments any of us have as human beings are those moments when for a little while it is possible to escape the squirrel-cage of being me into the landscape of being us.*
>
> — Frederick Buechner

Sometimes we would wonder if it was the best use of our time. But he would tell us that the most important thing we could do in life was to make these kids feel important."

Rich was able to make the kind of impact he had hoped for while he was there, and it appears that he knew in his heart that he would not be able to see that ministry to completion. Again Eric Hauck recalls, "The Tuesday before he died, Rich took me on a walk. He told me that he had just been down to the reservation, and he told me he had a mysterious experience while he was there. He said he saw a great ministry on the reservation, with lots of camps for the young people to teach them music and about the gospel. But then he started to cry, and he said to me, 'Eric, I really feel that God does not want me to be the one to make these ministries happen. God has not given me the freedom to do it. He has given me the ability to raise funds in order for others to make it possible. But I am not the one who will do it.' I knew that in his heart he really wanted to see that happen more than anything in the world."

After Rich's death, his brother, David, along with Alyssa Loukota, joined to continue Rich's work, particularly among the Native Americans. They formed a nonprofit organization called The Legacy of A Kid Brother of St. Frank. Rich was right. He would not be able to do the work himself, but others would rise up to carry on the vision.

Warming or Chilling the World

Rich once wrote, "We are joined in a responsibility to together make this world a good one for all of us. Each of us warms the world or chills it inasmuch as we offer or withhold respect, hospitality, encouragement, love, or truth. In that sense we are all parts of each other's well-being or sickness, and we affect the climate that we all share."[15] Saint John of the Cross said, "At the end of our life, we shall be judged by love." In his life and even in his death, by being his brothers' keeper, Rich made the world a few degrees warmer.

10

That Where I Am, There You May Also Be

Meditating on Death and the Life to Come

Live like you'll

die tomorrow,

Die knowing you'll

live forever

Rich Mullins spoke and sang a lot about death. He once said, "Sooner or later, we all die. . . . Never forget that someday you'll be dead. Because that's just as sure as anything I can think of."[1] It seems morbid to think about, but for Rich it was a strangely comforting thought. Because he knew that God is good, he believed death might not be the terrible thing we fear so much. He saw it instead as a certainty to embrace, and he was struck by the fact that no matter how rich or beautiful or intelligent we are, we will die. Death is the great equalizer.

There is only one thing I know I am going to do in my life. I don't know if I'll be a success, a failure, married, single—but I do know that sooner or later, I'm going to die. The finality of that is kind of like God's little joke. No matter how cool you think you are, you will decompose. Most people live most of their lives ignoring death. Anything that will remind us, we remove from sight. This obsession with immortality is a bizarre thing. What that tells me, though, is we must be immortal.[2]

We Are All Going to Die

In his song "I See You," Rich sang,
> *Well, the grass will die*
> *And the flowers fall*
> *But your Word's alive*
> *And it will be after all*

And in another song called "Be with You," Rich and his friend, Justin Peters, wrote:

Everybody each and all
We're gonna die eventually
It's no more or less our fault
Than it is our destiny

He looked at the rhythms of life and saw that death is an integral part of them. Rich was honest about death, as he was with every other part of our lives. He was never glib, or too happy, about a subject that frightens most people; he was realistic. And even more, he viewed death through the eyes of faith.

> *If I find in myself a desire which no experience in this world can satisfy, the most probable explanation is that I was made for another world.*
>
> — C. S. Lewis

What we wrestle with in our lives comes out in our words. This is even more true of writers. Rich wrestled with mortality, with life's ultimate meaning, and therefore they emerged in his lyrics. When asked what song among those he wrote was his favorite, without hesitation Rich always said, "Elijah," which is a song about his own death.

Elijah

The Jordan is waiting for me to cross thru
My heart is aging I can tell
So Lord, I'm begging for one last favor from You
Here's my heart—take it where You will

This life has shown me how we're mended and how we're torn
How it's O.K. to be lonely as long as you're free

Sometimes my ground was stoney
And sometimes covered up with thorns
And only You could make it what it had to be and now that it's done
If they dressed me like a pauper or if they dined me like a prince
If they lay me with my fathers or if my ashes scatter on the wind
I don't care

There's people been friendly,
But they'd never be your friends
Sometime this has bent me to the ground
But now that this is all ending
I want to hear some music once again
'Cause it's the finest thing that I have ever found

But the Jordan is waiting,
Though I ain't never seen the other side
Still they say you can't take in the things you have here
So on the road to salvation, I stick out my thumb
And He gives me a ride
And His music is already falling on my ears

There's people been talking, they say
They're worried about my soul
Well, I'm here to tell you I'll keep rocking
Till I'm sure it's my time to roll
And when I do

When I leave I want to go out like Elijah
With a whirlwind to fuel my chariot of fire
And when I look back on the stars
It'll be like a candlelight in Central Park
And it won't break my heart to say goodbye

Rich realized that all of the people he loved, and in fact, all of the people he knew, would die within a generation or two. He found this a sobering fact. It takes away our pride.

The truth is, everyone I know is going to be dead in the next thirty to forty years, so what's the big deal? You kinda shrug your shoulders, and you say, "After you've been dead a few years, it isn't going to make a difference." The thing about being forty is it's not as surprising to me as it used to be. I used to think about death a lot, and it was always a little bit intimidating to think about. Now I know a lot of dead people. It's not as big a deal as it used to be, but maybe because I'm not the one who died. I'm the one who's still living.[3]

Playing in the Graveyard

All around us are signs of death: cemeteries by the roadside, obituary columns, and the faces of loved ones long gone that sit atop our mantle. Most of us choose to turn away and say things like, "Life goes on." Rich could not easily turn away from something so deep and so real as death. Many people do not think about death until they reach middle age, but Rich's recognition of mortality started when he was a young boy. Amy Grant recalls, "One conversation that was very vivid to me was the time he told me about his little brother who died. I remember Rich telling me what it was like to sneak in and look at his empty crib and how it made him aware of death at an early age."

Rich learned from his family that death was not something to fear. His sister, Sharon Roberts, remembers having family picnics in a graveyard near their home and says, "We never thought it was strange. I think it taught us not to be so bothered by death." The image of small children playing—even having a picnic—in a cemetery is at first shocking, but when we view death in light of the Christian faith, it begins to make sense. Death is something we ought to befriend. According to the Christian faith, death is not the end but the beginning of life.

Rich understood this, and he was not afraid of his own death. His column about turning forty reveals that once he even suspected he might die at a young age.

In my mid- to late twenties I had some romantic, highly exaggerated notions about an early death—taking off at 33—joining the company of Mozart, . . . Jesus, and other immortals who checked out in their early thirties. But this was a party I didn't get an invitation to—a gang I didn't belong in (me not being a genius and all). So, in Chicago I

had my own party—celebrating the fun of being alive as opposed to the mystique of having an untimely death.[4]

LORD, *let me know my end, and what is the measure*

of my days; let me know how fleeting my life is.

You have made my days a few handbreadths,

and my lifetime is as nothing in your sight.

Surely everyone stands as a mere breath.

Surely everyone goes about like a shadow.

Surely for nothing they are in turmoil;

they heap up, and do not know who will gather.

And now, O LORD, what do I wait for?

My hope is in you.

— P s a l m   3 9 : 4 - 7

Rich was not cavalier about death; he was just certain of it, and this awareness freed him from fear. One of his friends and fellow artists, Carolyn Arends, comments, "Rich really understood that we are all terminal, and he didn't spend his time storing up treasures on earth. I don't think he spoke a lot about death because he knew he was going to die; he just knew that we were *all* going to die . . . someday, maybe sooner, maybe later."

This conviction helped Rich keep his life in perspective. "In terms of the scope of eternity," he said, "I really believe that we are dust. I really believe that I will someday be dead no matter how good my songs are. Someday I will decay. I will rot and there will be nothing left."[5] Rich saw clearly what Jesus meant in his parable about the rich man who stores up his wealth and smiles at his good fortune, only to die that same night. The punchline is obvious.

Though Rich always had a keen sense of the reality of death, it was even more clear after his mentor, Maurice Howard, died. Kathy Sprinkle remembers how important this was for Rich: "We had all just moved to Wichita, and we went on a sixteen-week tour before starting our lives there. Maurice died nine weeks into the tour. We found out about his death on our way to a concert in Philadelphia. That night, at the end of his concert, Rich took the microphone, and in a mournful, gut-wrenching moment, he sang the old hymn, 'This World Is Not My Home' for the first time. I will never forget it. Rich never looked at life and death the same way after Maurice's death."

> *Blessed be God for our sister, the death of the body.*
> — Saint Francis of Assisi

While death is imminent and unavoidable, it is not the end. This world is not our home. One of the best things about being a Christian is that we believe that death is not the end, that death has lost its sting, because Jesus has risen from the dead and we will rise with him. In the end, death becomes something not to fear but to embrace.

Free to Live

Embracing his own death was something else Rich learned from Saint Francis:

Francis reminded himself daily that he would be dead. . . . I think that while we live, the one sure thing about being alive is that we will die. Everything else is kind of "iffy." I mean, you may be rich, you may be poor. You may have a job tomorrow, you may not. Nothing is sure in life except that you will be dead. There's something really great about living in the awareness that we will someday die. For one thing, that makes all that is hard about life more endurable because we know it will pass. So I think that it teaches us to not hold on to things, to live with some sort of detachment. Not the sort of detachment where we are un-

moved, but the sort of detachment where we allow ourselves to be moved easily and quickly, but we don't try to possess those things that move us.[6]

This understanding of death, instead of paralyzing him with fear, actually freed Rich to live, to try things without a fear of failure, to let go of the things of this earth, and love people without expectations.

To live strongly and creatively, we must have firmly fixed in our minds that this life is not the end. Rich learned how our future can be incorporated into our life now. It is easy for us to become disappointed with our lives, to act as if our successes and failures in this life are all that matters. What we fail to realize is that the vast majority of our lives are before us. Coming to the end of this life, the life "in the flesh," is of little significance. Our death is really our birthday into God's full world.[7] This is because, in reality, we will never die. Rumors of our death are greatly exaggerated. In reality, we have gone on. Christians do not die. They simply change their residence.

> *When all of the suns and nebulae have passed away, each one of you will still be alive.*
>
> — C. S. Lewis

Thinking seriously about our death, instead of being morbid and frightening, should lead us into a greater freedom to live this life with abandon, curiosity, enthusiasm, and without fear. What do we have to lose, really? Rich perceived this more clearly than most of us. Many of us are preparing to live rather than actually living. Meditating upon our own death may awaken us to the fact that we have one life to live, and the day—the moment—we are in will never be repeated. In a sense, a well-lived life is the best way to cheat death. Rich put it well:

Once you come to understand that life is unbelievably brief and that we really can't do anything that's gonna change anything, that we don't really amount to a hill of beans—then all of a sudden you go, "So it doesn't really matter if I'm not great. And if I don't have to be great, that means I can fail. And if I can fail, that means I can try. And if I can try, that means I'm gonna have a good time."[8]

When we adopt this perspective, we become free. Life becomes less serious, and we are allowed to experiment and try new things without being afraid of how it will turn out. This attitude changes everything. Suddenly we are not encumbered by the need to succeed in everything we do. We are free to be real. We are free to enjoy life in all of its beauty instead of being hung up on what others think of us, or how well our career is going. In the end the size of our bank accounts and our waistlines will not matter.

Because of his grasp of death, Rich lived life with a kind of abandon that most of us can only admire, not imitate. While many worry about health or beauty and panic at the signs of aging, Rich saw the larger picture and embraced the life he had as a great gift. He said, "I plan on living to be eighty and I figure I'm not even halfway there. People say it's not fair that people should die when they are eighteen. I go, 'Wow, it's unfair that we should be able to live until we are that old.'"[9]

Rich could say this because he believed that none of us deserve anything. He saw us all as recipients of God's handouts. Whether life is short or long, he believed, it is still a gift. Living with this attitude prevented him from being obsessive about the things of this world. Rich said, "I just figure we're all gonna be dead someday anyway. You may as well go one way as the other. If you're overly obsessive about health, then you're dead already."[10]

Instead of worrying—which is the bane of our existence—Rich was free to enjoy each day. He understood what Jesus meant when He said, "Do not worry about your life. . . . Can any of you by worrying add a single hour to your span of life? . . . So do not worry about tomorrow, for tomorrow will bring worries of its own. Today's trouble is enough for today" (Matt. 6:25, 27, 34).

Jesus told us not to worry because worrying is useless. It cannot change anything, but it can surely ruin our chances of living and loving freely. To many, Rich seemed to live too recklessly; they wanted him to be a little more cautious, a little more tame. In retrospect it seems he was living with a ruthless trust in the goodness of God, and this way of seeing the world allowed him to enjoy it to the fullest.

In the play, *Our Town,* by Thornton Wilder, a young woman lay dying with her grieving family standing over her. In one of the most powerful scenes, she is allowed to look at her world one last time before moving on to heaven. She utters these wonderful and moving words: "Good-bye world . . . Good-bye to clocks ticking . . . and Mama's sunflowers. And food and coffee. And new-ironed dresses and hot baths . . . and sleeping and waking up. Oh, earth, you're too wonderful for anybody to realize you." The world is too wonderful for us to realize while we are living it.

> *I can never lose one whom I have loved unto the end. My beloved, the one to whom my soul cleaves so firmly that it can never be separated, does not go away but only goes before. Be mindful of me when you get to heaven, my friend, for I shall soon follow you.*
>
> — S a i n t   B e r n a r d   o f   C l a i r v a u x

Because he saw that life was short and should be enjoyed, Rich savored it. He drank a can of soda, for example, chugging and slurping like it was ambrosia, sometimes in a single gulp. He could consume an entire meal in a few minutes, finishing with a big smile on his face. He once said in a concert, "Don't you get sick of health freaks? I always want to say, 'Look, bud, you're gonna die anyway. You may as well go out eating something that you like. What is the point of living to be a hundred and fifty if all you get to eat is bean sprouts?'"[11]

Perhaps Rich lived carelessly, but he could never be accused of cheating himself out of all that life had to offer. During one of his last concerts, he admitted, "I abused myself as much as possible in the last twenty years. Which is fine with me. 'Cause I figure, sooner or later, life's gonna kill us all—you may as well go out doing something you love to do. Or eating something that you like to eat. Like cholesterol. . . . So go out and live real good, and I promise you'll be beat up real bad. But a little while after you're dead, you'll be rotted away anyway. . . . It's not gonna matter if you had a few scars. It will matter if you didn't live."[12]

Free to Love

Awareness of death made Rich not only free to live but free to love. His brother, David, remembers, "The realization that we are all going to die, Rich thought, made each day count more. He thought it could allow you to hurt." Rich himself didn't want to be caught at death having neglected the people in his life. He knew that the ability to love is precious and a sign that we have overcome death. John the apostle wrote, "We know that we have passed from death to life because we love one another" (1 John 3:14). The time we have is short, and it may be that we will not be able to tell others how much we love them until it is too late. Knowing this, Rich told audiences, "Love each other as much as you can right now because this may be the last day you've got to love each other. Don't love each other because you think you'll be less lonely if you do. There's no point in that. And don't try to get even, don't waste a lot of time trying to get even with each other because you never really do."[13]

When our lives are through, we will regret only that we loved too little, never that we loved too much. We withhold love in this life because we are afraid of being hurt. Rich was able to get beyond this fear.

Much of the time we think, "But if I love others, I will be vulnerable; I will appear weak; I may get hurt." Rich saw how short this life is and said, "Remember, someday you'll be dead. It won't last forever. So while you still have life, love everybody you can love. Love them as much as you can love them. Love freely."[14]

Rich also knew that he never really lost the people he loved. He strongly embraced the thought of the great fourth-century writer, John Cassian, who once wrote, "The bond between friends cannot be broken by chance; no interval of time or space can destroy it. Not even death itself can part true friends."

Mitch McVicker says of Rich, "As long as he was living, he wanted to live as fully as he could, because he often said that many people die long before their death." It was for this reason that Rich sang the song, "Live Right":

So don't hold out, don't let these chances pass you by
Here's your life, you're gonna get it right
Live like you'll die tomorrow
Die knowing you'll live forever, live right

Love like you'll leave tomorrow
Believing love lasts forever, live right

Rich certainly did that. He lived like he would die tomorrow, and he died knowing he would live forever.

That One Is Mine

Rich believed that at the moment of death believers are attended by the angels and taken up to be with Jesus. Rich spoke a lot about this in his concerts, and he used a story about Irish fishermen to convey his point.

When people come back from Ireland, they have those great big huge sweaters that have stitches and stuff in 'em, and all these designs. Well, those designs were made by fishermen's wives who began to knit for them these sweaters. And they would knit little charms and prayers into the sweaters. So then, if the charms and prayers "took," then the men would come back alive, and if they didn't—because fish don't eat wool—they could tell one husband from the other.

But . . . when life is done with you, when you wash up "over there," them angels . . . will look at what's left of your body and say, "Man, what is this?"

And Jesus will say, "Oh, I know who that is. That one is Mine!"

And the angel will say, "How do you know he's yours?"

And Jesus will say, "Well—you see that sweater they've got on? . . . I knit that for them."[15]

Rich believed that those who accepted Jesus' life and death, those who chose to follow Him by "putting on His sweater" (trusting in Jesus), would be rescued at death and received into everlasting life with Jesus. Death, for Rich, was only a moment; in the twinkling of an eye he would be transformed and resurrected into a new life. Death would not have the final word.

The Chariot of Fire

On September 19, 1997, Rich and Mitch McVicker loaded up Rich's jeep and headed to Wichita to play at a youth rally. They had spent the last three weeks recording Mitch's album and both were exhausted. It was sometime after 9:00 P.M. when they left the Chicago area. Not long into the drive they stopped at a gas station to get some coffee. Mitch recalls, "It was one of those coffee machines where you push a button and it fills the cup you put underneath it. It worked fine for me, but when Rich hit the button, the coffee just kept coming and wouldn't stop. It spilled over his cup and out onto the floor. The manager came rushing over as the coffee was spilling everywhere, and he looked at Rich and said, 'Excuse me, but are you Rich Mullins?' We laughed for the next ten minutes about that."

> *When we come to the end of a thing we have come to the beginning of it.*
>
> — G. K. Chesterton

They got back into the jeep and resumed the drive. It was dark and beginning to rain. The roads were becoming slick. Sometime around 10:00 P.M. the jeep drifted onto the grassy center median and was abruptly turned back onto the road, but the quick change of direction forced the jeep to lose its balance and it went into a roll. Neither Rich nor Mitch was wearing a seat belt, and both were thrown from the vehicle, which was traveling at about seventy miles per hour. A man driving a tractor trailer, as well as two women traveling in a car not far behind them, stopped when they came upon the wreckage. One of the women, a nurse, rushed to the bodies and discovered that Rich had died. Mitch was covered in blood and had endured a massive head injury but was still breathing.

The world would wake up to the news that Rich Mullins was dead and Mitch McVicker was in critical condition. Slowly, radio stations across the country started announcing the news. I was in Dallas, Texas, that weekend, performing a wedding ceremony when I found out what had happened. Late that night, I went alone to a field. The sky was thundering and raining, and the wind was blowing over me. I fell to my knees and cried until my sides hurt. I looked up at the angry sky and shouted to Rich, "Are you OK? Are you OK?"

In the whisper of the wind I heard his voice say, "I am OK . . . I am more than OK."

Mitch had been rushed to a hospital in Peoria, Illinois. My wife and I left immediately to be at his side. I was allowed to be with Mitch for a few moments while he was in intensive care. The doctors refused to predict if he would live, and even then, what kind of life he might have. I prayed for him and anointed him with oil. As news of the accident spread from coast to coast, thousands across the country offered prayers for Mitch's recovery. In a few weeks, Mitch was able to leave the hospital to begin the long process of rehabilitation.

Rich's funeral was held a few days after the accident and following the private memorial service, he was buried near his father. The next day many contemporary Christian recording artists attended a public service in Nashville. A few days later, another public memorial service was held in Wichita. In all, more than five thousand people came from several states to honor Rich.

After the funeral and the two memorial services, what seemed like a bad dream to Rich's many fans and friends was becoming a reality: Rich was really gone. It happened so unexpectedly and abruptly that it had seemed unreal. I kept expecting him to walk into the room any minute. In those days I reflected on the fact that Rich always said that he wanted "to go out like Elijah" in a "chariot of fire." In a sense, I thought, he did.

A few nights after Rich died, my son, Jacob, who was only five at the time, crawled into my lap. Sad because he saw me crying, he said, "It's OK, Dad. Uncle Rich is all right. The angels came and got him." His faith moved me to smile and cry at the same time. I wondered where Jacob had heard about angels coming and getting him. I had never told him that this is what happens at our death. Maybe he just knew it. "Yes," I said, "I suppose you're right, Jacob. The angels did come and get him. And maybe I will be happy about that tomorrow, but right now I am just sad because I won't get to see him again for a while." Everything Rich had said about death and heaven came rushing into my mind. The thing he had always talked about, the thing he had desired so much, had come to pass. He was where he always longed to be.

In My Father's House

Rich firmly believed that Jesus was telling the truth when He said He was preparing a place for us to live with Him forever (John 14:2–3). In one of his final songs, Rich sang of the joy of life in heaven.

That Where I Am, There You . . .

In my Father's house there are many, many rooms . . .
And I'm going up there now to prepare a place for you
That where I am there you may also be

If I go prepare a place for you, I will come back again . . .
You know I am the Way, the Truth, the Life—keep my command
That where I am there you may also be

That where I am, there you may also be
Up where the Truth—the Truth will set you free
In the world you will have trouble but I leave you my peace
That where I am there you may also be

Remember you did not choose me—no I have chosen you . . .
The world will show you hatred, the Spirit show you truth
That where I am, there you may also be

I've come down from the Father—time for me to go back up . . .
One command I leave you—love as I have loved
That where I am there you may also be

That where I am, there you may also be
Up where the Truth—the Truth will set you free
In the world you will have trouble but I leave you my peace
That where I am there you may also be

Rich trusted Jesus and His promise of everlasting life. In the song, we are comforted by the notion that Jesus cares enough for us to "prepare a place" where, presumably, we will really enjoy being. And it is a place altogether different from this world. In this world we will have "trouble;" in this world we will be shown a lot of "hatred." He firmly believed that when we are in heaven, we will know only peace and love.

There are some who believe that the Christian view of heaven is merely wishful thinking, an escape from reality. Rich commented on this by saying,

I used to make fun of the sentimental feeling of the church that
there was an afterlife. I used to mock songs about heaven. And I used to

Blessed be the God and Father of our Lord Jesus Christ!
By his great mercy he has given us a new
birth into a living hope through the resurrection
of Jesus Christ from the dead, and into an
inheritance that is imperishable, undefiled, and
unfading, kept in heaven for you.

— 1 P e t e r 1 : 3 - 4

think that it was somehow stupid and even wicked to dream of heaven
and to long for heaven. And now I see the kind of a horrible place earth
really is. I go hiking and I think, *This could be so beautiful.*

I met a guy last night sweeping the stairs. . . . down there. I talked
to this very gentle man, a very kind man, a very simple man, and I
thought, How could a world made up of people like this be such a horri-
ble place? And then I pick up the paper and read about dishonesty and
deceit and betrayal and all that and go, I *do* long for heaven.[16]

Longing for Heaven

According to the Bible, the life that awaits believers will be glorious. Life in heaven will be limitlessly enhanced. We will be more intensely alive than ever before. We will not sit idly or be put upon a shelf as one of God's trophy's, eternally collecting dust. No, we will be involved in endlessly interesting activities. If death creates the possibility of our finding this incredible life, Rich believed, then we ought not fear death, but look forward to it. This is why Rich said, "Saint Paul, I think, had the perfect take on the pluses and minuses of life and death—'to live is Christ, to die is gain.'"[17]

When someone we love dies, we have many questions: Where is he? What is she feeling? What is he doing now? Is she cold? Is he well? The problem is that when a person dies, they literally disappear from our sight. It is like when we were born. We came from nothing and suddenly existed; in death we are here and then suddenly gone.

> *We think of Eternal Life,*
> *if we think of it at all, as*
> *what happens when life ends.*
> *We would do better to think*
> *of it as what happens*
> *when life begins.*
> — Frederick Buechner

Death is really another birth. Imagine telling a baby in the womb, attached to an umbilical cord, "Hey, guess what? You are about to enter into a bright new world with sound and light and air and brilliant colors. You will be able to see and smell and taste for the first time. There are mountains and sunflowers and sandy beaches and . . . a lot of beautiful things out here. You're gonna have to let go of that umbilical cord. In fact, we're gonna snip it. Don't worry. You'll be fine after a few moments of crying." I think our death is something like that. It is actually a birth into a brighter, more aromatic, more delicious, more beautiful world than the one we now know. But we can only guess at it. We are really in no better position of understanding it than the infant could understand our world from the womb.[18]

I Believe in the Resurrection

One of the unique teachings of Christianity is that when we get to heaven we will not be floating spirits. We will be embodied. The idea of our being spirits who merely live in bodies now but will one day be set free of them actually came from the Greek philosophers, not the New Testament. Paul, in his first epistle to the Corinthians, revealed that believers will be resurrected, just as Jesus was, and will receive a body just as He did. It will be "a spiritual body" (1 Cor. 15:44), but it will be a body nonetheless.

Listen, I will tell you a mystery! We will not all die, but we will all be changed, in a moment, in the twinkling of an eye, at the last trumpet. For the trumpet will sound, and the dead will be raised imperishable, and we will be changed. For this perishable body must put on imperishability, and this mortal body must put on immortality. When this perishable body puts on imperishability, and this mortal body puts on immortality, then the saying that is written will be fulfilled: "Death has been swallowed up in victory." "Where, O death, is your victory? Where, O death, is your sting?"

— 1 C o r i n t h i a n s 1 5 : 5 1 - 5 5

In His resurrected state, Jesus had a tangible yet incorruptible, imperishable, and immortal body. In that body, Jesus ate fish for breakfast with the disciples on the beach; in that same body He walked right through a wall. Clearly, the believer's resurrected "container" will not be like anything we know on earth.

Rich liked this idea very much. He said, with both seriousness and humor,

Remember that after we die somehow, Christ is going to raise us up again, and somehow we'll be a body still. But we'll be different than we

are now. A new body's what we get—I've got a great one on order. You laugh, but someday you'll be astonished. I'll have no bags under my eyes, I'll have a jaw line, biceps—the whole works. I'll be a jock. Either a jock or a fife player, I haven't decided which.[19]

Though it is beyond our comprehension, it is exciting to think about what this new life will be like. Imagine no longer being under the burden of time and space and physical decay. This is why we should not grieve for the dead. They are now released from fear and loneliness and pain. They are finally home. They could not be in a better place. If we must be sad, we are sad for ourselves. But even that is only for a time.

Eternal Joy

What will heaven be like? Just as thinking seriously about our death—that this present life will end—enables us to live and love freely, so also thinking about heaven—that our real life will never end—can embolden us with hope, and ignite our enthusiasm. Think about Christmas morning. It is a day of great anticipation. We look forward to it all year. Why? Because on that morning we will do nothing except eat and open presents. In short, it is fun.

A lot of us have a very low and misguided view of heaven. If you ask many Christians what they think heaven will be like they say things like, "Well, I guess the streets will be made of gold . . . and we will all have wings . . . and we will all play a harp." Then you say, "Really. Do you like harp music?" And they say, "No. Not really." Many Christians have unwittingly adopted views about heaven that are less than inviting.

When we enter into heaven, we are entering a new kind of existence where there are no more tears; pain and suffering can never again come near us. But that is only the beginning. According to C. S. Lewis, there are five promises from the Bible that we have about heaven. First, we will be with Christ. Second, we will be like him, meaning, we will be whole and complete. Third, we will have glory—meaning, God will bless us; we will know the highest joy in the universe: "the satisfaction of having pleased" God. Fourth, we shall feast. The best Thanksgiving dinner will not be able to compare with this feast. And fifth, "we shall have some sort of official position in the universe."[20]

All of this is to say that what we will experience—what our loved ones as believers are now experiencing—is sheer delight. We will not only see beauty; we will become one with it; we will be infused by light and color. We will bathe in it. Lewis' last point, that "we shall have some sort of official position in the universe," is based on the verse in Revelation that

> *The bodies of God's people will therefore rise again, free from every defect, from every deformity, as well as from every corruption, encumbrance, or hindrance. In this respect their freedom of action will be as complete as their happiness.*
>
> — Saint Augustine

says, "And there will be no more night; they need no light of lamp or sun, for the Lord God will be their light, and they will reign forever and ever" (Rev. 22:5).

We will be doing something. To reign means to have say over something, to be in charge. We will be creating and building and organizing. We will not be sitting around doing nothing. George MacDonald imagined that we will be "lighting the moons" and clothing the world with greenery; we might even "hang gold sunsets over a rose and purple sea." We will be doing things that we love. In short, we will experience unending bliss.

Everything Will Return

For those of us who are still here while our loved ones have departed as Rich has, there is a pain and a sadness that seem unquenchable. Yet that anguish will lift—by degrees while we live on earth, completely when we reach heaven and see them again. The great writer, Vladimir Nabakov, touched on this truth in a letter he wrote to his mother three years after the death of his father. Even after three years she still felt the pain of her husband's death as if it were yesterday. He wrote the letter to encourage her and to help her through her times of mourning and loss.

"Three years have gone—and every trifle relating to father is still as alive as ever inside me. I am so certain, my love, that we will see him again, in an

> *"There are three experiences of bliss we shall have in heaven. First, the bliss of hearing God say, 'Well done.' Second, the bliss of having all of heaven hear it. And third, that this experience of bliss will last forever."*
>
> — B l e s s e d   J u l i a n   o f   N o r w i c h

unexpected but completely natural heaven, in a realm where all is radiance and delight. He will come toward us in our shared bright eternity, slightly raising his shoulders as he used to do, and we will kiss the birthmark on his hand without surprise. You must live in expectation of that tender hour, . . . and never give in to the temptation of despair. Everything will return."[21]

I am so eager for the day when I see Rich again. I imagine, like Nabakov, that when I see him in that realm of radiance and delight he will appear to me in a familiar way. Perhaps he will greet me with his marvelous laugh. Maybe I will catch a scent of patchouli. Everything will, indeed, return. Nothing that is good has been or ever will be lost.

Until that day I will think often of something Rich himself wrote about his life in heaven, and I will let it give me, in the words of one of his songs, "hope to carry on."

Someday I shall be a great saint—like those you see in the windows of magnificent cathedrals. I will have a soul made of sunlight and skin as clear as the stained glass panels that make their skin, and I will shine

like they do now. . . . Someday I will rise up like the sun in the morning—someday I will shine like the saints who watch from cathedral windows. I know this, not because of any evidence I have produced of myself, but because of the witness of His Scriptures, because of the evidence of His grace, and because of the testimony of this sky that washes over me at dusk.[22]

Until the day when I see my friend who now shines with the rest of the saints, I will remember that he is well. I will be happy for him. And I will rejoice in the knowledge that I will see him again.

aFTErword

When I heard the story that opens the introduction of this book, where Ben Pearson caught Rich in a pose he likened to an arrow pointing to heaven, I believed that was an appropriate picture of Rich's life. In many ways, he was an arrow that pointed to heaven. As you have read this book, I hope you have come to know more about Rich and what he believed. My greatest desire is that by reading this book you have also been pointed to God. Rich was used by God to inspire and challenge many people. I hope you have been inspired while reading this book.

The first time I met Jim Smith was at Rich's funeral. Rich had mentioned to both Jim and me that we should meet. He thought that we would really like each other and get along well. Since the funeral, we have had the opportunity to spend some time together. We have found that Rich was right. So when our family decided to allow a book to be written about Rich, Jim was the first person we felt should write it. We really appreciate the way Jim has handled writing about Rich. We feel he has written with honesty and integrity. We are thankful for the friendship that Rich had with Jim and his family and for the friendships we now have.

The Legacy

God gave a vision to Rich to share His love with Native Americans. Rich spent the last three years of his life calling Window Rock, Arizona, home. He moved to Window Rock to live among the Navajo people. He wanted to learn what life looked like from a pastoral people, a people similar to the pastoral Israelites. During his time there, he began formulating a plan to teach music and art to Native Americans. He wanted to teach and live out the love of Christ among them. He shared his ideas with several friends.

After Rich died, God planted in the hearts of our family and some of Rich's friends the desire to continue working toward the vision Rich had shared with us. In August 1998, a kickoff was held in Wichita for The Legacy of A Kid Brother of St. Frank, a nonprofit organization that seeks to open opportunities in the arts and music to Native Americans in the love of Christ and the example of Saint Francis.

The Legacy of A Kid Brother of St. Frank was established by pooling the resources of our family and many of Rich's friends. Alyssa Loukota, who had worked with Rich in the Southwest, knew a great deal of his plans and shared his passion for Native America. She contacted Jim Dunning Jr., Rich's accountant and business manager. At that time, our family was talking to Jim about our desire to see the work continued. Jim helped pull it all together, and Rich's board (which had helped guide Rich in his decision for his ministry) agreed to continue as our first board of directors. Other friends have also helped in supporting The Legacy from the beginning.

The Legacy has tried to follow the vision that Rich had for the work. While we are working to stay focused on the heart of the vision, we are primarily concerned with where God will lead us and to bring hope to a people that need it. Saint Francis said, "Go into all the world and preach the gospel; use words when necessary." We believe the best way to share the good news is to live out the love of Christ unconditionally.

We take our example from the Savior. Jesus, in healing the lame man, said to him, "Take up your mat and go." Jesus did not say to him, "As long as you use those legs to follow Me, they will bear you up and be strong." We believe that Jesus' lack of condition for His healing says, "I hope that My healing your legs will show you that I am the Son of God. I hope that My healing your legs will show you that I can heal your soul. My desire is that you will use those legs to walk after Me. If you choose not to believe in Me and to follow Me, enjoy your legs. Run, dance, jump—enjoy them. I can do more for you than heal your legs, but if that is all you will take from Me, you are welcome to it."

The Legacy seeks to teach music and the arts in the unconditional love of Christ. Through our lives and teaching, we hope the young people we work with will come to see a Savior who is worthy of praise. We hope they will use the music and arts they are taught to praise God. That is the best hope that can be found. If they choose to learn only to paint, bead, or play the guitar and decide not to serve Christ, we hope they enjoy the arts.

The Legacy of A Kid Brother of St. Frank works through partnering with other ministries to Native Americans. The programs we make available include weekend and weeklong camps that expose youth to various forms of the arts as well as equip them with techniques.

Legacy Retreats

Rich was used by God to reach many people and to strengthen their faith. Many people were challenged by the life and wisdom that Rich had of God and now desire to live a life of reckless abandon to Christ. The Legacy is working to continue to model and challenge the church to that kind of life. Weekend retreats are being taught around the country by The Legacy that focus on spiritual development.

It is encouraging to see how God will take the life of an individual and use that life to challenge and build the kingdom. And it is interesting to me that in the Bible God sometimes chose to implement His plan through the lives of several people. He would begin a ministry in one servant and bring it to fulfillment through another. We see that in Moses and Joshua. Moses led the people of Israel out of Egypt and through the wilderness wanderings; Joshua then led the people into the promised land. I also see it in the lives of Elijah and Elisha, and Paul and Barnabas. Paul points out that God works in this way. He tells the Corinthians that some plant, some water, but it is God who brings the increase (1 Cor. 3:6).

The work is God's. He may have chosen to use Rich to begin a work and another to finish it. He may begin a work in a preacher and finish it in a coal miner. Though we often do not see or understand all of God's ways, He is good, and He will work to bring good in all things. We miss Rich, but the things that he modeled and taught will live on because they were not his only, they were from God, who is the same yesterday, today, and forever.

David MULLINS

For more information about The Legacy organization and its retreats, contact:

The Legacy of A Kid Brother of St. Frank
303 N. Hillside, Wichita, KS 67214
Telephone (316) 612-4649, Fax (316) 612-4651
www.kidbrothers.org or kidbros@southwind.net

gROWing deeper
*Questions, Ideas, and
Exercises for Personal
or Group Reflection*

Chapter 1: First Family

Questions for Reflection

1. Think for a moment about your own lineage. Try to imagine your ancestors three generations back. What did they look like, where did they live, and what did they do? Do you think it is possible that they even dreamed of your existence one day in the future?

2. Listen to the song "First Family." What line is most meaningful for you? Explain why.

3. Describe your upbringing. What were your parents like? How did they shape you? How, if at all, are you becoming more like them?

4. What are some of the things you give thanks for about your family, your up-bringing, and the things that shaped you as you grew up?

5. Do you have any moments that you can remember when your family gave your faith "hands and feet"? When they gave it wings?

Ideas and Exercises

· Make a family tree by listing all of the ancestors you can. You may need to call an older relative to help you find some information, or you might try using the Internet or some other ancestry service to help you do this. Once you have drawn your tree, look it over, and make it an occasion for prayer. Give thanks for all of the lives that came together to make your life possible.

· Write a letter to your parents, thanking them for all that they gave to you. Do not spend time opening up old wounds; keep it positive, and focus on the things they did right.

Chapter 2: Creed

Questions for Reflection

1. What does the word *church* mean to you?

2. Listen to the song "Creed." What line is most meaningful for you? Explain why.

3. Think about your own church heritage. What denomination did you grow up in? If you became a Christian as an adult, what denomination are you a part of now? What particularly draws you to this denomination?

4. Rich spoke about how the church is designed to "make" us. What part of the church—the music, hymns, the prayers, the liturgy, Communion, the sermon—seems to give you the most encouragement and inspiration at this stage in your journey?

5. What areas would you like to see your own church improve upon? How can you be involved to make that happen?

Ideas and Exercises

• Memorize the Apostle's Creed or the Nicene Creed. Let these ancient truths of the faith begin to mold and shape the way you see the world.

• Write a letter of encouragement to a leader in your local church, perhaps your pastor. Let the person know how much his or her hard work has meant to you.

Chapter 3: The Love of God

Questions for Reflection

1. How would you rate yourself in terms of how certain you are that God loves you: *I don't believe it; I struggle with believing it; I am beginning to believe it; I believe that God loves me despite my failures and sins; I live with complete confidence in God's love, and I live with radical trust.* Explain why.

2. Listen to the song "The Love of God." What line is most meaningful for you? Explain why.

3. How does the love you experienced from your parents affect the way you feel about God's love toward you?

4. Which of the three ways we see God's love (creation, Jesus, and the love of others) has been the most meaningful for you?

5. What people in your life have "put a face on grace," making God's love real to you? Explain.

Ideas and Exercises

• Memorize 1 John 4:10, 19.

• Be a "face of grace" for someone this week. Find someone who doubts God's personal love (there are many) and share the good news of God's relentless and unconditional passion for him or her.

Chapter 4: Boy Like Me/Man Like You

Questions for Reflection

1. What part of Jesus' humanity—that He was once a small boy, that He was able to laugh and weep, that He suffered and felt all of the pain you do—is the most encouraging to you?

2. Listen to the song "Boy Like Me/Man Like You." What line is most meaningful for you? Explain why.

3. How do you understand the person of Jesus as being fully God and fully man? Do you find it hard to comprehend? Explain.

4. After reading this chapter, how—if at all—do you think differently about Jesus from the way you did before?

5. Rich said he wanted to grow up and be like Jesus. What parts of Jesus' life do you find the easiest, and the most difficult, to imitate? Explain.

Ideas and Exercises

· Read a section from one of the Gospels each day for a week. Pay attention to the person of Jesus. Notice what He does, not just what He says. Try to picture Him in your mind getting in boats, going up a mountain to pray, attending a wedding. As best you can, try to actually enter the scene. Walk alongside Jesus in this way for a few moments each day.

· Try Rich's personal discipline of staying up an extra hour before sleeping in order to be with Jesus. Don't make it overly spiritual. Just be with Him as a friend who is sitting in the room with you. (You might want to start with 15 minutes if an hour seems too much.)

Chapter 5: Calling Out Your Name

Questions for Reflection

1. Describe your relationship with nature. Has it always been meaningful? Do you prefer the city and being indoors? Do you find more beauty in the mountains? the plains? the ocean?

2. Listen to the song "Calling Out Your Name." What line is most meaningful for you? Explain why.

3. What about the created world—the beauty, the order, the wildness, the vastness, the complexity—teaches you the most about God?

4. Describe a time when you sensed that "the heavens" were "declaring the glory of God."

5. God calls us not only to enjoy creation but also to create. What kinds of things do you create? How do you feel when you are doing it?

Ideas and Exercises

· Try to learn the names of the trees on your block. If you don't know the names, ask someone who might, or check out a tree-identification book from the library.

· One of Rich's goals was to chart the movements of the Big Dipper. Pay attention to the stars for one week. Step outside for a few moments before going to bed just to look at the sky (and realize that the world is a lot bigger than you).

Chapter 6: Bound to Come Some Trouble

Questions for Reflection

1. What do you think about the belief that if you love God and are faithful, then your life will be free of pain and suffering? Can you think of any biblical examples of this?

2. Listen to the song "Bound to Come Some Trouble." What line is most meaningful for you? Explain why.

3. What are some of the most difficult struggles you have had in your life?

4. Rich said that one of the hardest parts about being a Christian is surrendering to God and trusting that He will take care of us. Describe yourself in terms of your ability to trust God even when things look bleak.

5. Amy Grant said that Rich was able to go "into the abyss," come back out, and write a song. How has your own personal struggle deepened you, made you more aware of others, or allowed you to be helpful to others who are suffering?

Ideas and Exercises

· Make an inventory of your own struggles from the past. Write down how God has been faithful through those times. Use this list as a reason to give thanks to God.

· Do you know someone who is struggling right now? If so, give him or her a call or write a note. Try not to offer cheap encouragement by saying things like, "It'll pass." Instead, let him or her know that God is close, and so are you.

Chapter 7: My One Thing

Questions for Reflection

1. Why do you think our culture is so fascinated with money? What are some examples that prove our world is driven by the desire for wealth?

2. Listen to the song "My One Thing." What line is most meaningful for you? Explain why.

3. How would you describe yourself in terms of the way you see money and material possessions: *I try to earn all I can and buy all I can; I like to have nice things; I can take it or leave it; I don't care much about money or material possessions; I enjoy things, but they are not what is most important to me.* Explain.

4. How does your church leadership talk about money? Do they encourage people to be wealthy as a sign of God's blessing? Do they encourage members to de-accumulate as a way to be free? Do they encourage people to give to the church or to the poor? After reading this chapter, how do you feel about what your leadership is teaching?

5. Rich was able to be free not only of the desire to have wealth but also of the desire to be successful. Describe yourself in terms of your desire to be a success. How has this chapter influenced your understanding of what it means to be a success?

Ideas and Exercises

· Take a weekend to de-accumulate. Go through your house and see if there are things you don't need. Give these things away, perhaps to the Salvation Army or some other organization, to distribute them to the poor.

· It was said in this chapter that we buy things we don't need in order to impress people we do not even like. Try to make your next purchases with this in mind. Ask, *Do I really need this, or am I buying it because I think it will enhance my status?*

· What talent do you have? Do you treat it as a gift from God? Use it today as a means of service and blessing to someone.

Chapter 8: Growing Young

Questions for Reflection

1. Why do we tend to think that ministers and Christian celebrities are somehow beyond being tempted?

2. Listen to the song "Growing Young." What line is most meaningful for you? Explain why.

3. Rich sings, "We have sinned and grown old," meaning that when we run from God into sin we age, but when we repent and return to God we "grow young." What is it about sin that "ages" us?

4. It was said in this chapter that Rich tried hard to "starve" the seven deadly sins (pride, envy, anger, sloth, greed, gluttony, and lust). If you are comfortable answering this, describe which of the seven you are starving, and which ones you tend to feed.

5. Rich was very open about his struggles because, as he said, if God knew his sins, then why shouldn't someone else? Who are the people you feel most comfortable sharing your struggles with? Explain.

Ideas and Exercises

· Meditate on the seven deadly sins. Ask God to help you "starve" (meaning, give no opportunities for or make no provision for) the ones that give you the most trouble.

· Find a friend or a small group of people with whom you can speak honestly about your struggles with sin and temptation. Be sure that the person is trustworthy, aware of his/her own sinfulness, and able to keep confidential what you share.

Chapter 9: Brother's Keeper

Questions for Reflection

1. If it is true that the world will know that we are Jesus' disciples by our love for one another, how well do you think we are doing? Rate the church on a scale from one to ten. Explain your rating.

2. Listen to the song "Brother's Keeper." What line is most meaningful for you? Explain why.

3. Rich believed that an important part of loving others is simply not judging them. How have you been unfairly judged? How have you unfairly judged others?

4. Who are some of the people who have really loved you despite your flaws? How do they show their love?

5. Rich said that real love is not feeling, but doing; it is not just in talking about loving others, it is doing the ordinary things in life with faithfulness. How would you describe yourself in terms of acting out your love for God and others?

Ideas and Exercises

• Go a day without judging anyone. See if you can refrain from looking down on others, and instead pray for sensitivity to see the pain in other people's lives.

• Do a good deed. Pray that God would bring someone your way whom you can serve or bless. Be careful, this prayer always gets answered.

Chapter 10: That Where I Am, There You May Also Be

Questions for Reflection

1. How do you think about death? Is it something you would rather not think about, something you have thought more about recently, something you are afraid of?

2. Listen to the song "That Where I Am, There You. . . ." What line is most meaningful for you? Explain why.

3. Why did Rich find death so freeing? Is it freeing to you?

4. The fact that we all die seemed to make Rich more insistent that we love as freely and fully as we can because the time is short. If you knew you had three days to live, what kinds of things would you want to do with your remaining time?

5. What are your views of heaven? After reading this chapter, have they been changed?

Ideas and Exercises

• Write your own obituary. What kinds of things do you want said about you when you are gone? Think of ways you can begin becoming that kind of person.

• Saint Paul said, "To live is Christ, to die is gain." Make a list of all of the things you are looking forward to doing or being in heaven.

Introduction

1. Light Music Tribute Special, 1997.

Chapter 1

1. Jim Long, "Excuse Me, Are You Rich Mullins?" *Campus Life*, February 1994.
2. *20: The Countdown Magazine* tribute special, 18 November 1997.
3. Ibid.
4. Rich Mullins concert, Wheaton College, 15 September 1990.
5. Holly Halverson, "A Ragamuffin's Oz," *CCM* magazine, December 1993.
6. From the author's recollection of a personal conversation with Rich Mullins.
7. Brian Q. Newcombe, "Step by Step: A Conversation with Rich Mullins," *CCM* magazine, June 1992.
8. Les Sussman, *Praise Him! Christian Music Stars Share Their Favorite Verses from Scripture* (New York: St. Martin's Press, 1998), 155–64.
9. Radio interview with Artie Terry, "The Exchange," WETN, Wheaton College, April 1997.
10. Ibid.
11. Newcombe, "Step by Step."
12. *Homeless Man: The Restless Heart of Rich Mullins* video (Word Entertainment, 1998).
13. Rich Mullins concert, Anderson, Ind., 16 November 1995.
14. Radio interview with Artie Terry, "The Exchange," April 1997.
15. Radio interview with Brian Beatty, Creation Festival Radio Special, Mt. Union, Pa., 27 June 1996.
16. *ReleasExtra*, 1994.

Chapter 2

1. Rich Mullins concert, Anderson, Ind., 16 November 1995.
2. Brian Q. Newcombe, "Step by Step: A Conversation with Rich Mullins," *CCM* magazine, June 1992.
3. Interview in *Christianity Online*, September 1995.
4. *CCM* magazine tribute issue, November 1997.
5. Rich Mullins, "A Message to the Media," Creation Festival Radio Special, Mt. Union, Pa., 27 June 1996.
6. *CCM* tribute issue.
7. Holly Halverson, "A Ragamuffin's Oz," *CCM* magazine, December 1993.

8. G. K. Chesterton, *Orthodoxy* (San Francisco: Ignatius Press, 1995), 13.

9. C. S. Lewis, "Membership," *The Weight of Glory and Other Addresses* (New York: Simon & Schuster, 1996), 129.

10. *20: The Countdown Magazine* tribute special, 18 November 1997.

11. From the transcript of a video taken during a worship service in his brother David Mullins's church in West Virginia, 1995.

12. *20: The Countdown Magazine* tribute special.

13. *Homeless Man: The Restless Heart of Rich Mullins* video (Word Entertainment, 1998).

14. Rich Mullins, "The World As Best As I Remember It," booklet with album.

15. Holly Halverson, "A Ragamuffin's Oz," *CCM* magazine, December 1993.

16. *20: The Countdown Magazine* tribute special.

17. Christopher Lee Coppernoll, *Soul 2 Soul* (Nashville: Word Publishing, 1998), 49.

18. Lighthouse Music tribute special, 1997.

19. Rich Mullins concert, Taylor University, Upland, Ind., 21 September 1996.

20. Radio interview with Artie Terry, "The Exchange," WETN, Wheaton, Ill., April 1997.

21. Ibid.

Chapter 3

1. Rich Mullins concert, Joy Jam, Louisville, Ky., 1994.

2. *20: The Countdown Magazine* tribute special, 18 November 1997.

3. Peter G. Van Breemen, *As Bread That Is Broken* (Dimension Press, 1981), 11.

4. *ReleasExtra*, "Another Mile Farther Down the Road," 1994.

5. Rich Mullins concert, Joy Jam, Louisville, Ky.

6. Rich Mullins, "Joking Matters," *Release* magazine, January/February 1996.

7. Tony Cummings, "The Last Words of a Ragamuffin," *Release* magazine, August/September 1998.

8. *Rich Mullins: Pursuit of a Legacy* video (Nashville: Reunion Records, 1994).

9. Les Sussman, *Praise Him! Christian Music Stars Share Their Favorite Verses from Scripture* (New York: St. Martin's Press, 1998), 155–64.

10. Radio interview, "True Tunes," Wheaton, Ill., 15 September 1990.

11. Rich Mullins concert, Joy Jam, Louisville, Ky.

12. William Blake, "The Little Black Boy."

13. Sussman, *Praise Him!*, 155–64.

14. Rich Mullins, "The Divine Obsession," *Release* magazine, September/October 1995.

15. Rich Mullins concert, Anderson, Ind., 16 November 1995.

16. Rich Mullins, "A Message to the Media," Creation Festival Radio Special, Mt. Union, Pa., 27 June 1996.

17. *CCM* magazine tribute issue, November 1997.

18. Interview by Thom Granger, "Hope to Carry On," *CCM* magazine, May 1990.

Chapter 4

1. Rich Mullins, "Invisible Things," *Release* magazine, November/December 1994.
2. Interview by Brendt Waters, *Lighthouse* magazine, April 1996.
3. *20: The Countdown Magazine* tribute special, 18 November 1997.
4. I am indebted to a wonderful Christmas Eve sermon delivered by Bishop Basil at St. George Orthodox Church in Wichita, Kan., for these marvelous images, which I have paraphrased.
5. *CCM* magazine tribute issue, November 1997.
6. Rich Mullins concert, Anderson, Ind., 16 November 1995.
7. Les Sussman, *Praise Him! Christian Music Stars Share Their Favorite Verses from Scripture* (New York: St. Martin's Press, 1998), 155–64.
8. Rich Mullins concert, Taylor University, Upland, Ind., 21 September 1996.
9. For further reading on this see Chris Kettler, *The Vicarious Humanity of Christ and the Reality of Salvation* (Lanham, Md.: University Press of America, 1991).
10. Rich Mullins, "Considering the Lilies," *Release* magazine, Summer 1991.
11. Sussman, *Praise Him!*, 155–64.
12. *Homeless Man: The Restless Heart of Rich Mullins* video (Word Entertainment, 1998).
13. Radio interview with Bob Michaels, Light 99, KTLI, Wichita, Kan., for the premiere of *Canticle of the Plains*, 2 February 1997.
14. Anne Lamott, *Traveling Mercies* (New York: Pantheon Books, 1999), 134.
15. Sussman, *Praise Him!*, 155–64.

Chapter 5

1. *20: The Countdown Magazine* tribute special, 18 November 1997.
2. Rich Mullins, "Pictures in the Sky," *Release* magazine, May/June 1995.
3. Rich Mullins, "Boats and Burning Bushes," *Release* magazine, Winter 1993.
4. From two separate occasions, a Rich Mullins concert, Wheaton, Ill., 15 September 1990, and the *Rich Mullins: Pursuit of a Legacy* video (Nashville: Reunion Records, 1994).
5. Rich Mullins, "Washing at Dusk," *Release* magazine, Summer 1992.
6. Holly Halverson, "A Ragamuffin's Oz," *CCM* magazine, December 1993.
7. G. K. Chesterton, *Orthodoxy* (San Francisco: Ignatius Press, 1995), 65–66.
8. William Blake, "Auguries of Innocence."
9. "Music and More," radio interview for Compassion International, 1993.
10. Rich Mullins, "A Message to the Media," Creation Festival Radio Special, Mt. Union, Pa., 27 June 1996.
11. Christopher Lee Coppernoll, *Soul 2 Soul* (Nashville: Word Publishing, 1998), 100.
12. *CCM* magazine tribute issue, November 1997.
13. Coppernoll, *Soul 2 Soul*, 100–101.
14. *CCM* magazine tribute issue.
15. Ibid.
16. I was given a copy of this special letter by Rich's close friend, Kathy Sprinkle.
17. *ReleasExtra*, 1994.

Chapter 6

1. "Music and More," radio interview, Compassion International, 1993.
2. Jack W. Hill, "Singer Seeks Other Take on Christianity," *Arkansas Democrat-Gazette*, September 1995.
3. Phil Newman, "Where Mercy Leads," *Release* magazine, 10 September 1995.
4. *20: The Countdown Magazine*, interview, January 1995.
5. From an unpublished source.
6. Radio interview with Artie Terry, "The Exchange," WETN, Wheaton College, April 1997.
7. *ReleasExtra*, 1994.
8. *20: The Countdown Magazine* tribute special, 18 November 1997.
9. Ibid.
10. *CCM* magazine tribute issue, November 1997.
11. *Homeless Man: The Restless Heart of Rich Mullins* video (Word Entertainment, 1998).
12. Ibid.
13. Cornerstone '97, July 1997.
14. Interview with Linda Thompson Stonehocker, *The Phantom Tollbooth*, February 1997.
15. Rich Mullins, "The World as Best as I Remember It," booklet with album.
16. Brian Q. Newcombe, "Step by Step: A Conversation with Rich Mullins," *CCM* magazine, June 1992.
17. Rich Mullins concert, Green Bay, Wis., 10 August 1997.
18. Radio interview by Brian Beatty, Creation Festival Radio Special, Mt. Union, Pa., 27 June 1996.
19. *20: The Countdown Magazine* tribute special.
20. Brian Rhinehart, concert review, Anderson University, Anderson, Ind., 16 November 1995.

Chapter 7

1. Interview with Linda Thompson Stonehocker, *The Phantom Tollbooth*, February 1997.
2. Brian Q. Newcombe, "Step by Step: A Conversation with Rich Mullins," *CCM* magazine, June 1992.
3. I am indebted to Richard Foster and Arthur G. Gish for this succinct and very accurate indictment of our culture.
4. I am once again indebted to Richard Foster and his chapter "Simplicity," *Celebration of Discipline* (San Francisco: HarperSanFrancisco, 1978). See the revised edition, p. 83, for his comments on this. Foster makes the point that while Jesus' main message concerned the kingdom of God, his primary social concern had to do with money. He gives several examples worth looking at.
5. Melinda Scruggs, "Rich Mullins: Songs of Another Kind," *CCM* magazine, January 1986.
6. *Homeless Man: The Restless Heart of Rich Mullins* video (Word Entertainment, 1998).

7. "Music and More," radio interview, Compassion International, 1993.

8. Quoted from Rich's memorial service in Wichita, Kan.

9. *CCM* magazine tribute issue, November 1997.

10. Lou Carlozo, "Christian Rocker Finds New Life in the Desert," *Chicago Tribune*, 25 April 1996.

11. Rich Mullins, "A Message to the Media," Creation Festival Radio Special, Mt. Union, Pa., 27 June 1996.

12. *CCM* magazine tribute issue.

13. Radio interview with Bob Michaels, Light 99, KTLI, Wichita, Kan., for the premiere of *Canticle of the Plains*, 2 February 1997.

14. *ReleasExtra*, 1994.

15. Ibid.

Chapter 8

1. Rich told this story many times. It is excerpted here from Jim Long, "Excuse Me, but Aren't You Rich Mullins?" *Campus Life*, February 1994.

2. "Music and More," radio interview, Compassion International, 1993.

3. Rich Mullins concert, Green Bay, Wis., 10 August 1997.

4. *20: The Countdown Magazine* tribute special, 18 November 1997.

5. Les Sussman, *Praise Him!: Christian Music Stars Share Their Favorite Verses from Scripture* (New York: St. Martin's Press, 1998), 155–164.

6. "Music and More" interview.

7. Christopher Lee Coppernoll, *Soul 2 Soul* (Nashville: Word Publishing, 1998), 211.

8. *Rich Mullins: Pursuit of a Legacy* video (Nashville: Reunion Records, 1994).

9. Rich Mullins, "Virtue Reality," *Release* magazine, July/August 1994.

10. *Pursuit of a Legacy* video.

11. Sussman, *Praise Him!*, 155–64.

12. Ibid.

13. Interview by Brendt Waters, *Lighthouse* magazine, April 1996.

14. Ibid.

15. From an e-magazine interview, James Long, *CCM*, November 1995.

Chapter 9

1. Christopher Lee Coppernoll, *Soul 2 Soul* (Nashville: Word Publishing, 1998), 121–22.

2. Rich Mullins, "Virtue Reality," *Release* magazine, July/August 1994.

3. Rich Mullins concert, Taylor University, Upland, Ind., 21 September 1996.

4. *CCM* magazine tribute issue, November 1997.

5. Mullins, "Joking Matters," *Release* magazine, January/February 1996.

6. Mullins, "Virtue Reality."

7. *20: The Countdown Magazine* tribute special, 18 November 1997.

8. Rich Mullins, "A Message to the Media," Creation Festival Radio Special, Mt. Union, Pa., 27 June 1996.

9. Robyn Frazer, "Mullin' Things Over," *CCM* magazine, April 1987.
10. *Homeless Man: The Restless Heart of Rich Mullins* video (Word Entertainment, 1998).
11. "Music and More" radio interview, Compassion International, 1993.
12. *Homeless Man* video.
13. Ibid.
14. Ibid.
15. Rich Mullins, "Never Alone," *Release* magazine, March/April 1996.

Chapter 10

1. Rich Mullins concert, Taylor University, Upland, Ind., 21 September 1996.
2. Frazer, "Rich Mullins: Mullin' Things Over," *CCM* magazine, April 1987.
3. Interview with Linda Thompson Stonehocker, *The Phantom Tollbooth*, February 1997.
4. Rich Mullins, "The Big 4-Oh," *Release* magazine, November/December 1995.
5. *20: The Countdown Magazine* tribute special, 18 November 1997.
6. *CCM* magazine tribute issue, November 1997.
7. I am indebted to my friend and mentor, Dallas Willard, for this clear teaching on death and heaven. For further study, see his book, *The Divine Conspiracy* (San Francisco: HarperSan Francisco, 1998).
8. Radio interview with Brian Beatty, Creation Festival Radio Special, Mt. Union, Pa., 27 June 1996.
9. *20: The Countdown Magazine* tribute special.
10. *CCM* magazine tribute issue.
11. Rich Mullins concert, Green Bay, Wis., 10 August 1997.
12. *Homeless Man: The Restless Heart of Rich Mullins* video (Word Entertainment, 1998).
13. Rich Mullins concert, Taylor University.
14. Ibid.
15. *Homeless Man* video.
16. *20: The Countdown Magazine* tribute special.
17. Mullins, "The Big 4-Oh."
18. I am indebted to John O'Donohue for this metaphor, in his excellent book, *Anam Cara: A Book of Celtic Wisdom* (New York: HarperCollins, 1997).
19. Rich Mullins concert, Taylor University.
20. C. S. Lewis, "The Weight of Glory," *The Weight of Glory and Other Addresses* (New York: Simon & Schuster, 1996), 131.
21. Willard, *The Divine Conspiracy*, 85. He took the quote from *Books & Culture*, November/December 1995.
22. Mullins, "Washing at Dusk," *Release* magazine, Summer 1992.

s O N G   l i s t

Chapter 1

"First Family" by Rich Mullins, © 1989 BMG Songs, Inc. (ASCAP), *Never Picture Perfect* (Nashville: Reunion, 1989).

Chapter 2

"Creed" by Rich Mullins and Beaker, © 1993 BMG Songs, Inc. (ASCAP) and Kid Brothers of St. Frank Publishing (ASCAP), *A Liturgy, A Legacy and a Ragamuffin Band* (Nashville: Reunion , 1993). All rights on behalf of Kid Brothers of St. Frank Publishing administered by BMG Songs, Inc.

"Step by Step" by Beaker, © 1991 BMG Songs, Inc. and Kid Brothers of St. Frank Publishing (ASCAP), *The World as Best as I Remember It, Volume One* (Nashville: Reunion, 1991). All rights on behalf of Kid Brothers of St. Frank Publishing administered by BMG Songs, Inc.

"Alrightokuhhuhamen" by Rich Mullins, © 1990 BMG Songs, Inc. (ASCAP), *Never Picture Perfect* (Nashville: Reunion, 1989).

"While the Nations Rage" by Rich Mullins, © 1990 BMG Songs, Inc. (ASCAP), *Never Picture Perfect* Nashville: Reunion, 1989).

"The Just Shall Live" by Rich Mullins, © 1992 BMG Songs, Inc. (ASCAP), *The World as Best as I Remember It, Volume Two* (Nashville: Reunion, 1992).

Chapter 3

"The Love of God" by Rich Mullins, © 1990 BMG Songs, Inc. (ASCAP), *Never Picture Perfect* (Nashville: Reunion, 1991).

"To Tell Them" by Rich Mullins, © 1992 BMG Songs, Inc. (ASCAP), *The World as Best as I Remember It, Volume Two* (Nashville: Reunion, 1992).

"All the Way to Kingdom Come" by Rich Mullins, © 1998 Liturgy Legacy Music (ASCAP), *The Jesus Record* (Nashville: Myrrh, 1998).

"If I Stand" by Rich Mullins and Steve Cudworth, © 1988 BMG Songs, Inc. (ASCAP), *Winds of Heaven, Stuff of Earth* (Nashville: Reunion, 1988).

"Nothing Is Beyond You" by Rich Mullins, Mitch McVicker, and Dana Waddel, © 1998 Liturgy Legacy Music (ASCAP), *The Jesus Record* (Nashville: Myrrh, 1998).

Chapter 4

"Boy Like Me/Man Like You" by Rich Mullins and Beaker, © 1991 BMG Songs, Inc. and Kid Brothers of St. Frank Publishing (ASCAP), *The World as Best as I Remember It, Volume One* (Nashville: Reunion, 1991). All rights on behalf of Kid Brothers of St. Frank Publishing administered by BMG Songs, Inc.

"All the Way to Kingdom Come" by Rich Mullins, © 1998 Liturgy Legacy Music (ASCAP), *The Jesus Record* (Nashville: Myrrh, 1998).

"Hard" by Rich Mullins, © 1993 BMG Songs, Inc. (ASCAP), *A Liturgy, A Legacy and a Ragamuffin Band* (Nashville: Reunion, 1993).

"Jesus" by Rich Mullins, © 1998 Liturgy Legacy Music (ASCAP), *The Jesus Record* (Nashville: Myrrh, 1998).

Chapter 5

"Calling Out Your Name" by Rich Mullins, © 1990 BMG Songs, Inc. (ASCAP), *The World as Best as I Remember It, Volume One* (Nashville: Reunion, 1991).

"Pictures in the Sky" by Rich Mullins, © 1987 BMG Songs, Inc. (ASCAP), *Pictures in the Sky* (Nashville: Reunion, 1987).

"I See You" by Rich Mullins, © 1991 BMG Songs, Inc. (ASCAP), *The World as Best as I Remember It, Volume One* (Nashville: Reunion, 1991).

"Here in America" by Rich Mullins, © 1991 BMG Songs, Inc. (ASCAP), *A Liturgy, A Legacy and a Ragamuffin Band* (Nashville: Reunion, 1993).

"With the Wonder" by Rich Mullins, © 1988 BMG Songs, Inc. (ASCAP), *Winds of Heaven, Stuff of Earth* (Nashville: Reunion, 1988).

Chapter 6

"Bound to Come Some Trouble" by Rich Mullins, © 1990 BMG Songs, Inc. (ASCAP), *Never Picture Perfect* (Nashville: Reunion, 1989).

"Verge of a Miracle" by Rich Mullins, © 1987 BMG Songs, Inc. (ASCAP), *Pictures in the Sky* (Nashville: Reunion, 1987).

"The Agony and the Glory" by Rich Mullins, Keith Thomas, Mike Hudson, and Pam Mark Hall, © 1985 BMG Songs, Inc. (ASCAP), Straightway Music Co., (ASCAP), and Word Music Co. (ASCAP). Recorded by Pam Mark Hall, *Supply and Demand* (Nashville: Reunion, 1984).

"Damascus Road" by Rich Mullins and Beaker, © 1996 BMG Songs, Inc. and Kid Brothers of St. Frank Publishing (ASCAP), *Brother's Keeper* (Nashville: Reunion, 1995). All rights on behalf of Kid Brothers of St. Frank Publishing administered by BMG Songs, Inc.

Chapter 7

"My One Thing" by Rich Mullins, © 1990 BMG Songs, Inc. (ASCAP), *Never Picture Perfect* (Nashville: Reunion, 1989).

"Hard" by Rich Mullins, © 1993 BMG Songs, Inc. (ASCAP), *A Liturgy, A Legacy and a Ragamuffin Band* (Nashville: Reunion, 1993).

"This World is Not My Home" by J. R. Baxter, © 1937, Albert E. Brumley.

Chapter 8

"Growing Young" by Rich Mullins and Beaker, © 1992 BMG Songs, Inc. and Kid Brothers of St. Frank Publishing (ASCAP), *The World as Best as I Remember It, Volume Two* (Nashville: Reunion, 1992). All rights on behalf of Kid Brothers of St. Frank Publishing administered by BMG Songs, Inc.

"Waiting" by Rich Mullins and Beaker, © 1992 BMG Songs, Inc. and Kid Brothers of St. Frank Publishing (ASCAP), *The World as Best as I Remember It, Volume Two* (Nashville: Reunion, 1992). All rights on behalf of Kid Brothers of St. Frank Publishing administered by BMG Songs, Inc.

"Hold Me Jesus" by Rich Mullins, © 1999 BMG Songs, Inc. (ASCAP), *A Liturgy, A Legacy and a Ragamuffin Band* (Nashville: Reunion, 1993).

Chapter 9

"Brother's Keeper" by Rich Mullins and Beaker, © 1996 BMG Songs, Inc. and Kid Brothers of St. Frank Publishing (ASCAP), *Brother's Keeper* (Nashville: Reunion, 1995). All rights on behalf of Kid Brothers of St. Frank Publishing administered by BMG Songs, Inc.

"Peace (A Communion Blessing from St. Joseph's Square)" by Rich Mullins and Beaker, © 1993 BMG Songs, Inc. and Kid Brothers of St. Frank Publishing (ASCAP), *A Liturgy, A Legacy and a Ragamuffin Band* (Nashville: Reunion, 1993). All rights on behalf of Kid Brothers of St. Frank Publishing administered by BMG Songs, Inc.

"A Place to Stand" by Rich Mullins, © 1985 BMG Songs, Inc. (ASCAP), *Rich Mullins* (Nashville: Reunion, 1986).

Chapter 10

"That Where I Am, There You May Also Be" by Rich Mullins, © 1998 Liturgy Legacy Music and Word Music, Inc. (ASCAP), *The Jesus Record* (Nashville: Myrrh, 1998).

"I See You" by Rich Mullins, © 1991 BMG Songs, Inc. (ASCAP), *The World as Best as I Remember It, Volume One* (Nashville: Reunion, 1991).

"Can I Be With You" by Rich Mullins and Justin Peters, © 1987 BMG Songs, Inc. (ASCAP) and River Oaks Music (ASCAP), *Pictures in the Sky* (Nashville: Reunion, 1987).

"Elijah" by Rich Mullins, © 1983 Meadowgreen Music Company (ASCAP), *Rich Mullins* (Nashville: Reunion, 1986).

"Live Right" by Rich Mullins, Reed Arvin, and Wayne Kirkpatrick, © 1985 BMG Songs, Inc. (ASCAP) and Careers-BMG Music Publishing, Inc. (BMI), *Rich Mullins* (Nashville: Reunion, 1986).

C D   s O N G   l i s t

Permissions

"First Family"
"The Love of God"
"Calling Out Your Name"
"Bound to Come Some Trouble"
"My One Thing"
>All written by Richard Mullins
>BMG Songs, Inc. (ASCAP)

"Creed"
"Boy Like Me / Man Like You"
"Growing Young"
"Brother's Keeper"
>All written by Richard Mullins / Beaker
>BMG Songs, Inc. (ASCAP) / Kid Brothers of St. Frank Publishing
>All rights administered Worldwide by BMG Songs, Inc. (ASCAP)

"That Where I Am, There You May Also Be"
>Written by Rich Mullins
>US & Foreign: Word Music, Inc.
>US & Foreign: Liturgy Legacy Music (Administered
>by Word Music, Inc.)